CAMBRIDGE LIBRARY COLLECTION

Books of enduring scholarly value

English Men of Letters

In the 1870s, Macmillan publishers began to issue a series of books called
'English Men of Letters' – biographies of English writers by other English
writers. The general editor of the series was the journalist, critic, politician,
and supporter (and later biographer) of Gladstone, John Morley (1838–
1923). The aim was to provide a short introduction to each subject and his
works, but also that the life should illuminate the works, and vice versa. The
subjects range chronologically from Chaucer to Thackeray and Dickens, and
an important feature of the series is that many of the authors (Henry James
on Hawthorne, Ward on Dickens) were discussing writers of the previous
generation, and some (Trollope on Thackeray) had even known their subjects
personally. The series exemplifies the British approach to literary biography
and criticism at the end of the nineteenth century, and also reveals which
authors were at that time regarded as canonical.

Burke

This volume on Edmund Burke (1729–97), published in 1879 in the first
series of English Men of Letters, was written by the general editor of the
series, John Morley (1838–1923). Himself a politician as well as an author,
Morley had previously published a 'historical study' of Burke in 1867, but
emphasises in an introductory note that this book 'is biographical rather than
critical' and is intended as a narrative life. Morley himself was a radical in
politics, and his interest in Burke, whom he does not hesitate to characterise
on occasion as a narrow-minded reactionary, may seem surprising, but he
greatly admired his subject's independent political stance, which he describes
as a mixture of utilitarian liberalism and historic conservatism, unfettered
by abstract doctrine, and which he believed might again come to dominate
political discourse in the last decades of the nineteenth century.

T0370939

Cambridge University Press has long been a pioneer in the reissuing of out-of-print titles from its own backlist, producing digital reprints of books that are still sought after by scholars and students but could not be reprinted economically using traditional technology. The Cambridge Library Collection extends this activity to a wider range of books which are still of importance to researchers and professionals, either for the source material they contain, or as landmarks in the history of their academic discipline.

Drawing from the world-renowned collections in the Cambridge University Library and other partner libraries, and guided by the advice of experts in each subject area, Cambridge University Press is using state-of-the-art scanning machines in its own Printing House to capture the content of each book selected for inclusion. The files are processed to give a consistently clear, crisp image, and the books finished to the high quality standard for which the Press is recognised around the world. The latest print-on-demand technology ensures that the books will remain available indefinitely, and that orders for single or multiple copies can quickly be supplied.

The Cambridge Library Collection brings back to life books of enduring scholarly value (including out-of-copyright works originally issued by other publishers) across a wide range of disciplines in the humanities and social sciences and in science and technology.

Burke

JOHN MORLEY

CAMBRIDGE UNIVERSITY PRESS

Cambridge, New York, Melbourne, Madrid, Cape Town,
Singapore, São Paolo, Delhi, Mexico City

Published in the United States of America by Cambridge University Press, New York

www.cambridge.org
Information on this title: www.cambridge.org/9781108034746

© in this compilation Cambridge University Press 2011

This edition first published 1879
This digitally printed version 2011

ISBN 978-1-108-03474-6 Paperback

This book reproduces the text of the original edition. The content and language reflect
the beliefs, practices and terminology of their time, and have not been updated.

Cambridge University Press wishes to make clear that the book, unless originally published
by Cambridge, is not being republished by, in association or collaboration with, or
with the endorsement or approval of, the original publisher or its successors in title.

English Men of Letters

EDITED BY JOHN MORLEY

BURKE

BURKE

BY

JOHN MORLEY.

London:

MACMILLAN AND CO.

1879.

The Right of Translation and Reproduction is Reserved.

SIXTH THOUSAND.

NOTE.

THE present writer published a study on Burke some
twelve years ago. It was almost entirely critical, and in
no sense a narrative. The volume now submitted to the
readers of this Series is biographical rather than critical,
and not more than about a score of pages have been
reproduced in it from the earlier book. Three pages
(pp. 211—213) have been inserted from an article on
Burke contributed by me to the new edition of the
Encyclopædia Britannica ; and I have to thank Messrs.
Black for the great courtesy with which they have allowed
me to transcribe the passage here. These borrowings
from my former self, the reader will perhaps be willing
to excuse, on the old Greek principle, that a man may
once say a thing as he would have it said, δὶς δὲ οὐκ
ἐνδέχεται—he cannot say it twice.

J. M.

CONTENTS.

BURKE.

CHAPTER I.

EARLY LIFE, AND FIRST WRITINGS.

IT will soon be a hundred and twenty years since Burke first took his seat in the House of Commons, and it is eighty-five years since his voice ceased to be heard there. Since his death, as during his life, opinion as to the place to which he is entitled among the eminent men of his country has touched every extreme. Tories have extolled him as the saviour of Europe. Whigs have detested him as the destroyer of his party. One undiscriminating panegyrist calls him the most profound and comprehensive of political philosophers that has yet existed in the world. Another and more distinguished writer insists that he is a resplendent and far-seeing rhetorician, rather than a deep and subtle thinker. A third tells us that his works cannot be too much our study, if we mean either to understand or to maintain against its various enemies, open and concealed, designing and mistaken, the singular constitution of this fortunate island. A fourth, on the contrary, declares that it would be hard to find a single leading principle or prevailing sentiment in one half

of these works, to which something extremely adverse
cannot be found in the other half. A fifth calls him one
of the greatest men, and, Bacon alone excepted, the greatest
thinker, who ever devoted himself to the practice of English politics. Yet, oddly enough, the author of the fifth
verdict will have it that this great man and great thinker
was actually out of his mind, when he composed the
pieces for which he has been most widely admired and
revered.

A sufficient interval has now passed to allow all the
sediment of party fanaticism to fall to the bottom. The
circumstances of the world have since Burke's time undergone variation enough to enable us to judge, from many
points of view, how far he was the splendid pamphleteer
of a faction, and how far he was a contributor to the
universal stock of enduring wisdom. Opinion is slowly,
but without reaction, settling down to the verdict that
Burke is one of the abiding names in our history, not
because he either saved Europe or destroyed the Whig
party; but because he added to the permanent considerations of wise political thought, and to the maxims of
wise practice in great affairs, and because he imprints
himself upon us with a magnificence and elevation of
expression, that places him among the highest masters of
literature, in one of its highest and most commanding
senses. Those who have acquired a love for abstract politics amid the almost mathematical closeness and precision
of Hobbes, the philosophic calm of Locke or Mill, or even
the majestic and solemn fervour of Milton, are revolted by
the unrestrained passion and the decorated style of Burke.
His passion appears hopelessly fatal to success in the pursuit
of Truth, who does not usually reveal herself to followers
thus inflamed. His ornate style appears fatal to the

cautious and precise method of statement, suitable to matter which is not known at all unless it is known distinctly. Yet the natural ardour which impelled Burke to clothe his judgments in glowing and exaggerated phrases, is one secret of his power over us, because it kindles in those who are capable of that generous infection a respondent interest and sympathy. But more than this, the reader is speedily conscious of the precedence in Burke of the facts of morality and conduct, of the many interwoven affinities of human affection and historical relation, over the unreal necessities of mere abstract logic. Burke's mind was full of the matter of great truths, copiously enriched from the fountains of generous and many-coloured feeling. He thought about life as a whole, with all its infirmities and all its pomps. With none of the mental exclusiveness of the moralist by profession, he fills every page with solemn reference and meaning ; with none of the mechanical bustle of the common politician, he is everywhere conscious of the mastery of laws, institutions, and government over the character and happiness of men. Besides thus diffusing a strong light over the awful tides of human circumstance, Burke has the sacred gift of inspiring men to use a grave diligence in caring for high things, and in making their lives at once rich and austere. Such a part in literature is indeed high. We feel no emotion of revolt when Mackintosh speaks of Shakespere and Burke in the same breath, as being both of them above mere talent. And we do not dissent when Macaulay, after reading Burke's works over again, exclaims, "How admirable! The greatest man since Milton!"

The precise date of Burke's birth cannot be stated with certainty. All that we can say is that it took place either

in 1728 or 1729, and it is possible that we may set it down
in one or the other year, as we choose to reckon by the old
or the new style. The best opinion is that he was born at
Dublin on the 12th of January, 1729 (N.S.). His father
was a solicitor in good practice, and is believed to have
been descended from some Bourkes of county Limerick,
who held a respectable local position in the time of the
civil wars. Burke's mother belonged to the Nagle family,
which had a strong connexion in the county of Cork ; they
had been among the last adherents of James II., and they
remained firm Catholics. Mrs. Burke remained true to
the church of her ancestors, and her only daughter was
brought up in the same faith. Edmund Burke and his
two brothers, Garret and Richard, were bred in the religion of their father ; but Burke never, in after times,
lost a large and generous way of thinking about the more
ancient creed of his mother and his uncles.

In 1741 he was sent to school at Ballitore, a village
some thirty miles away from Dublin, where Abraham
Shackleton, a Quaker from Yorkshire, had established
himself fifteen years before, and had earned a wide reputation as a successful teacher and a good man. According
to Burke, he richly deserved this high character. It was
to Abraham Shackleton that he always professed to owe
whatever gain had come to him from education. If I am
anything, he said many years afterwards, it is the education I had there that has made me so. His master's skill
as a teacher did not impress him more than the example
which was every day set before him, of uprightness and
simplicity of heart. Thirty years later, when Burke
had the news of Shackleton's death (1771), "I had a
true honour and affection," he wrote, "for that excellent
man. I feel something like a satisfaction in the midst of

my concern, that I was fortunate enough to have him
once under my roof before his departure." No man has
ever had a deeper or more tender reverence than Burke
for homely goodness, simple purity, and all the pieties
of life; it may well be that this natural predisposi-
tion of all characters at once so genial and so serious
as his, was finally stamped in him by his first schoolmaster. It is true that he was only two years at Ballitore, but two years at that plastic time often build up
habits in the mind that all the rest of a life is unable to
pull down.

In 1743 Burke became a student of Trinity College,
Dublin, and he remained there until 1748, when he took
his Bachelor's degree. These five years do not appear to
have been spent in strenuous industry in the beaten paths
of academic routine. Like so many other men of great gifts,
Burke in his youth was desultory and excursive. He roamed
at large over the varied heights that tempt our curiosity,
as the dawn of intelligence first lights them up one after
another with bewitching visions and illusive magic. "All
my studies," Burke wrote in 1746, when he was in the
midst of them, "have rather proceeded from sallies of
passion, than from the preference of sound reason; and,
like all other natural appetites, have been very violent for
a season, and very soon cooled, and quite absorbed in the
succeeding. I have often thought it a humorous consideration to observe and sum up all the madness of this
kind I have fallen into, this two years past. First, I was
greatly taken with natural philosophy; which, while I
should have given my mind to logic, employed me incessantly. This I call my *furor mathematicus*. But this
worked off as soon as I began to read it in the college,
as men by repletion cast off their stomachs all they have

eaten. Then I turned back to logic and metaphysics.
Here I remained a good while, and with much pleasure,
and this was my *furor logicus*, a disease very common in
the days of ignorance, and very uncommon in these enlightened times. Next succeeded the *furor historicus*,
which also had its day, but is now no more, being entirely
absorbed in the *furor poeticus*."

This is from one of Burke's letters to Richard Shackleton, the son of his schoolmaster, with whom he had
formed one of those close friendships that fill the life of
generous youth, as ambition fills an energetic manhood.
Many tears were shed when the two boys parted at
Ballitore, and they kept up their intimacy by a steady
correspondence. They discuss the everlasting dispute as
to the ultimate fate of those who never heard the saving
name of Christ. They send one another copies of verses,
and Burke prays for Shackleton's judgment on an invo-
cation of his new poem, to beauteous nymphs who haunt
the dusky wood, which hangs recumbent o'er the crystal
flood. Burke is warned by Shackleton to endeavour to
live according to the rules of the Gospel, and he humbly
accepts the good advice, with the deprecatory plea that
in a town it is difficult to sit down to think seriously :
it is easier, he says, to follow the rules of the Gospel
in the country, than at Trinity College, Dublin. In the
region of profaner things the two friends canvass the
comparative worth of Sallust and of Tully's Epistles.
Burke holds for the historian, who has, he thinks, a
fine, easy, diversified narrative, mixed with reflection,
moral and political, neither very trite nor obvious, nor
out of the way and abstract, and this is the true beauty
of historical observation.

Some pages of verse describe to Shackleton how his

friend passes the day, but the reader will perhaps be
content to learn in humbler prose, that Burke rose with
the dawn, and strode forth into the country through
fragrant gardens and the pride of May, until want of
breakfast drove him back unwillingly to the town, where
amid lectures and books his heart incessantly turned to
the river and the fir woods of Ballitore.　In the evening
he again turned his back on the city, taking his way
" where Liffey rolls her dead dogs to the sea," along to
the wall on the shore, whence he delighted to see the sun
sink into the waters, gilding ocean, ships, and city as it
vanished.　Alas, it was beneath the dignity of verse to
tell us what we should most gladly have known.　For,

> " The muse nor can, nor will declare,
> What is my work, and what my studies there."

What serious nourishment Burke was laying in for his
understanding, we cannot learn from any other source.
He describes himself as spending three hours almost every
day in the public library, " the best way in the world,"
he adds oddly enough, " of killing thought."　I have
read some history, he says, and among other pieces of
history, " I am endeavouring to get a little into the
accounts of this, our own poor country,"—a pathetic
expression, which represents Burke's perpetual mood, as
long as he lived, of affectionate pity for his native land.
Of the eminent Irishmen whose names adorn the annals
of Trinity College in the eighteenth century, Burke
was only contemporary at the University with one, the
luckless sizar who in the fulness of time wrote the *Vicar
of Wakefield*.　There is no evidence that at this time he
and Goldsmith were acquainted with one another.　Flood
had gone to Oxford some time before.　The one or two

companions whom Burke mentions in his letters, are only
shadows of names. The mighty Swift died in 1745, but
there is nothing of Burke's upon the event. In the same
year came the Pretender's invasion, and Burke spoke of
those who had taken part in it in the same generous
spirit that he always showed to the partisans of lost
historic causes.

Of his own family Burke says little, save that in
1746 his mother had a dangerous illness. In all my
life, he writes to his friend, I never found so heavy a
grief, nor really did I well know what it was before.
Burke's father is said to have been a man of angry and
irritable temper, and their disagreements were frequent.
This unhappy circumstance made the time for parting not
unwelcome. In 1747 Burke's name had been entered at
the Middle Temple, and after taking his degree, he
prepared to go to England to pursue the ordinary course
of a lawyer's studies. He arrived in London in the early
part of 1750.

A period of nine years followed, in which the circumstances of Burke's life are enveloped in nearly complete
obscurity. He seems to have kept his terms in the regular
way at the Temple, and from the mastery of legal principles and methods which he afterwards showed in some
important transactions, we might infer that he did more
to qualify himself for practice than merely dine in the
hall of his Inn. For law, alike as a profession and an instrument of mental discipline, he had always the profound
respect that it so amply deserves, though he saw that it
was not without drawbacks of its own. The law, he said, in
his fine description of George Grenville, in words that all
who think about schemes of education ought to ponder,
" is, in my opinion, one of the first and noblest of human

sciences ; *a science which does more to quicken and invigo-rate the understanding than all the other kinds of learning put together ;* but it is not apt, except in persons very hap-pily born, to open and to liberalize the mind exactly in the same proportion."[1] Burke was never called to the bar, and the circumstance that, about the time when he ought to have been looking for his first guinea, he published a couple of books which had as little as possible to do with either law or equity, is a tolerably sure sign that he had followed the same desultory courses at the Temple as he had followed at Trinity College. We have only to tell over again a very old story. The vague attractions of literature prevailed over the duty of taking up a serious profession. His father, who had set his heart on having a son in the rank of a barrister, was first suspicious, then extremely indignant, and at last he withdrew his son's allowance, or else reduced it so low that the recipient could not possibly live upon it. This catastrophe took place some time in 1755,—a year of note in the history of literature, as the date of the publication of Johnson's Dictionary. It was upon literature, the most seductive, the most deceiving, the most dangerous of professions, that Burke, like so many hundreds of smaller men before and since, now threw himself for a livelihood.

Of the details of the struggle we know very little. Burke was not fond in after life of talking about his earlier days, not because he had any false shame about the straits and hard shifts of youthful neediness, but because he was endowed with a certain inborn state-liness of nature, which made him unwilling to waste thoughts on the less dignified parts of life. This is no unqualified virtue, and Burke might have escaped some

[1] *American Taxation.*

wearisome frets and embarrassments in his existence, if
he had been capable of letting the detail of the day lie
more heavily upon him. So far as it goes, however, it is
a sign of mental health that a man should be able to cast
behind him the barren memories of bye-gone squalor.
We may be sure that whatever were the external ordeals
of his apprenticeship in the slippery craft of the literary
adventurer, Burke never failed in keeping for his constant companions, generous ambitions and high thoughts.
He appears to have frequented the debating clubs in
Fleet Street and the Piazza of Covent Garden, and he
showed the common taste of his time for the theatre.
He was much of a wanderer, partly from the natural
desire of restless youth to see the world, and partly
because his health was weak. In after life he was a
man of great strength, capable not only of bearing the
strain of prolonged application to books and papers in
the solitude of his library, but of bearing it at the same
time with the distracting combination of active business
among men. At the date of which we are speaking, he
used to seek a milder air at Bristol, or in Monmouth-
shire, or Wiltshire. He passed the summer in retired
country villages, reading and writing with desultory
industry, in company with William Burke, a namesake
but perhaps no kinsman. It would be interesting to
know the plan and scope of his studies. We are practi-
cally reduced to conjecture. In a letter of counsel to his
son in after years, he gave him a weighty piece of advice,
which is pretty plainly the key to the reality and fruit-
fulness of his own knowledge. "*Reading*," he said, "*and
much reading is good. But the power of diversifying
the matter infinitely in your own mind, and of applying
it to every occasion that arises, is far better ; so don't*

suppress the vivida vis." We have no more of Burke's
doings than obscure and tantalizing glimpses, tantalizing, because he was then at the age when character
usually either fritters itself away, or grows strong on the
inward sustenance of solid and resolute aspirations.
Writing from Battersea to his old comrade, Shackleton,
in 1757, he begins with an apology for a long silence
which seems to have continued from months to years.
" I have broken all rules; I have neglected all decorums;
everything except that I have never forgot a friend,
whose good head and heart have made me esteem and
love him. What appearance there may have been of
neglect, arises from my manner of life; chequered with
various designs; sometimes in London, sometimes in
remote parts of the country; sometimes in France, and
shortly, please God, to be in America."

One of the hundred inscrutable rumours that hovered
about Burke's name was, that he at one time actually did
visit America. This was just as untrue as that he became a
convert to the Catholic faith; or that he was the lover of
Peg Woffington; or that he contested Adam Smith's chair
of moral philosophy at Glasgow along with Hume, and
that both Burke and Hume were rejected in favour of
some fortunate Mr. James Clow. They are all alike
unfounded. But the same letter informs Shackleton of a
circumstance more real and more important than any
of these, though its details are only doubtfully known.
Burke had married—when and where, we cannot tell.
Probably the marriage took place in the winter of
1756. His wife was the daughter of Dr. Nugent,
an Irish physician once settled at Bath. One story is
that Burke consulted him in one of his visits to the west
of England, and fell in love with his daughter. Another

version makes Burke consult him after Dr. Nugent had
removed to London ; and tells how the kindly physician,
considering that the noise and bustle of chambers over
a shop must hinder his patient's recovery, offered him
rooms in his own house.   However these things may have
been, all the evidence shows Burke to have been fortunate in the choice or accident that bestowed upon him
his wife.   Mrs. Burke, like her father, was, up to the time
of her marriage, a Catholic.   Good judges belonging to her
own sex describe her as gentle, quiet, soft in her manners,
and well-bred.   She had the qualities which best fitted and
disposed her to soothe the vehemence and irritability of
her companion.   Though she afterwards conformed to the
religion of her husband, it was no insignificant coincidence
that in two of the dearest relations of his life the atmo-
sphere of Catholicism was thus poured round the great
preacher of the crusade against the Revolution.

About the time of his marriage, Burke made his first
appearance as an author.   It was in 1756 that he published *A Vindication of Natural Society,* and the more important essay, *A Philosophical Inquiry into the Origin of
our Ideas on the Sublime and Beautiful.*   The latter of
them had certainly been written a long time before, and
there is even a traditional legend that Burke wrote it when
he was only nineteen years old.   Both of these performances have in different degrees a historic meaning, but
neither of them would have survived to our own day
unless they had been associated with a name of power.
A few words will suffice to do justice to them here.   And
first as to the *Vindication of Natural Society.*   Its alternative title was, *A View of the Miseries and Evils arising to
Mankind from every Species of Civil Society, in a Letter
to Lord* ——, *by a late Noble Writer.*   Bolingbroke had

died in 1751, and in 1754 his philosophical works were
posthumously given to the world by David Mallet, Dr. Johnson's beggarly Scotchman, to whom Bolingbroke had left
half-a-crown in his will, for firing off a blunderbuss which
he was afraid to fire off himself. The world of letters had
been keenly excited about Bolingbroke. His busy and
chequered career, his friendship with the great wits of the
previous generation, his splendid style, his bold opinions,
made him a dazzling figure. This was the late Noble
Writer whose opinions Burke intended to ridicule, by reducing them to an absurdity in an exaggeration of Bolingbroke's own manner. As it happened, the public did not
readily perceive either the exaggeration in the manner, or
the satire in the matter. Excellent judges of style made
sure that the writing was really Bolingbroke's, and serious
critics of philosophy never doubted that the writer, whoever he was, meant all that he said. We can hardly help
agreeing with Godwin, when he says that in Burke's
treatise the evils of existing political institutions, which
had been described by Locke, are set forth more at large,
with incomparable force of reasoning and lustre of eloquence, though the declared intention of the writer was
to show that such evils ought to be considered merely
trivial. Years afterwards, Boswell asked Johnson whether
an imprudent publication by a certain friend of his at an
early period of his life, would be likely to hurt him?
" No, sir," replied the sage ; " not much ; it might perhaps be mentioned at an election." It is significant that
in 1765, when Burke saw his chance of a seat in Parliament, he thought it worth while to print a second edition
of his *Vindication*, with a preface to assure his readers that
the design of it was ironical. It has been remarked as a very
extraordinary circumstance that an author who had the

greatest fame of any man of his day as the master of a
superb style, for this was indeed Bolingbroke's position,
should have been imitated to such perfection by a mere
novice, that accomplished critics like Chesterfield and
Warburton should have mistaken the copy for a first-
rate original. It is, however, to be remembered that the
very boldness and sweeping rapidity of Bolingbroke's
prose rendered it more fit for imitation, than if its merits
had been those of delicacy or subtlety; and we must
remember that the imitator was no pygmy, but himself
one of the giants. What is certain is that the study of
Bolingbroke which preceded this excellent imitation, left
a permanent mark, and traces of Bolingbroke were never
effaced from the style of Burke.

The point of the *Vindication* is simple enough. It is
to show that the same instruments which Bolingbroke
had employed in favour of natural against revealed religion, could be employed with equal success in favour of
natural as against, what Burke calls, artificial society.
" Show me," cries the writer, " an absurdity in religion,
and I will undertake to show you a hundred for one in
political laws and institutions. . . . . If, after all, you
should confess all these things, yet plead the necessity of
political institutions, weak and wicked as they are, I can
argue with equal, perhaps superior force, concerning the
necessity of artificial religion ; and every step you advance
in your argument, you add a strength to mine. So that if
we are resolved to submit our reason and our liberty to
civil usurpation, we have nothing to do but to conform as
quietly as we can to the vulgar notions which are connected with this, and take up the theology of the vulgar
as well as their politics. But if we think this necessity
rather imaginary than real, we should renounce their

dreams of society, together with their visions of religion, and vindicate ourselves into perfect liberty."

The most interesting fact about this spirited performance is, that it is a satirical literary handling of the great proposition which Burke enforced, with all the thunder and lurid effulgence of his most passionate rhetoric five-and-thirty years later. This proposition is that the world would fall into ruin, " if the practice of all moral duties, and the foundations of society, rested upon having their reasons made clear and demonstrative to every individual." The satire is intended for an illustration of what with Burke was the cardinal truth for men, namely, that if you encourage every individual to let the imagination loose upon all subjects, without any restraint from a sense of his own weakness, and his subordinate rank in the long scheme of things, then there is nothing of all that the opinion of ages has agreed to regard as excellent and venerable, which would not be exposed to destruction at the hands of rationalistic criticism. This was Burke's most fundamental and unswerving conviction from the first piece that he wrote down to the last, and down to the last hour of his existence.

It is a coincidence worth noticing that only two years before the appearance of the *Vindication*, Rousseau had published the second of the two memorable Discourses in which he insisted with serious eloquence on that which Burke treats as a triumph of irony. He believed, and many thousands of Frenchmen came to a speculative agreement with him, that artificial society had marked a decline in the felicity of man, and there are passages in the Discourse in which he demonstrates this, that are easily interchangeable with passages in the *Vindication*. Who would undertake to tell us from internal evidence whether the following

page, with its sombre glow, is an extract from Burke, or
an extract from the book which Rousseau begins by the
sentence that man is born free, yet is he everywhere in
chains ?—

There are in Great Britain upwards of a hundred thousand
people employed in lead, tin, iron, copper, and coal mines; these
unhappy wretches scarce ever see the light of the sun; they are
buried in the bowels of the earth ; there they work at a severe
and dismal task, without the least prospect of being delivered
from it ; they subsist upon the coarsest and worst sort of fare ;
they have their health miserably impaired, and their lives cut
short, by being perpetually confined in the close vapour of these
malignant minerals. A hundred thousand more at least are
tortured without remission by the suffocating smoke, intense
fires, and constant drudgery, necessary in refining and managing
the products of those mines. If any man informed us that two
hundred thousand innocent persons were condemned to so intolerable slavery, how should we pity the unhappy sufferers, and how
great would be our just indignation against those who inflicted
so cruel and ignominious a punishment ! . . . . But this number,
considerable as it is, and the slavery, with all its baseness and
horror, which we have at home, is nothing to what the rest of the
world affords of the same nature. Millions daily bathed in the
poisonous damps and destructive effluvia of lead, silver, copper,
and arsenic, to say nothing of those other employments, those
stations of wretchedness and contempt, in which civil society has
placed the numerous *enfans perdus* of her army. Would any
rational man submit to one of the most tolerable of these
drudgeries, for all the artificial enjoyments which policy has
made to result from them ? . . . . Indeed the blindness of one
part of mankind co-operating with the frenzy and villany of the
other, has been the real builder of this respectable fabric of
political society : and as the blindness of mankind has caused
their slavery, in return their state of slavery is made a pretence
for continuing them in a state of blindness; for the politician
will tell you gravely, that their life of servitude disqualifies the
greater part of the race of man for a search of truth, and supplies
them with no other than mean and insufficient ideas. This is but
too true ; and this is one of the reasons for which I blame such
institutions.

From the very beginning, therefore, Burke was drawn to the deepest of all the currents in the thought of the eighteenth century. Johnson and Goldsmith continued the traditions of social and polite literature which had been established by the Queen Anne men. Warburton and a whole host of apologists carried on the battle against deism and infidelity. Hume, after furnishing the arsenal of scepticism with a new array of deadlier engines and more abundant ammunition, had betaken himself placidly to the composition of history. What is remarkable in Burke's first performance is his discernment of the important fact, that behind the intellectual disturbances in the sphere of philosophy, and the noisier agitations in the sphere of theology, there silently stalked a force that might shake the whole fabric of civil society itself. In France, as all students of its speculative history are agreed, there came a time in the eighteenth century when theological controversy was turned into political controversy. Innovators left the question about the truth of Christianity, and busied themselves with questions about the ends and means of governments. The appearance of Burke's *Vindication of Natural Society* coincides in time with the beginning of this important transformation. Burke foresaw from the first what, if rationalism were allowed to run an unimpeded course, would be the really great business of the second half of his century.

If in his first book Burke showed how alive he was to the profound movement of the time, in the second he dealt with one of the most serious of its more superficial interests. The essay on the Sublime and Beautiful fell in with a set of topics, on which the curiosity of the better minds of the age, alike in France, England, and Germany was fully stirred. In England the essay has been ordinarily slighted;

C

it has perhaps been overshadowed by its author's fame
in weightier matters. The nearest approach to a full and
serious treatment of its main positions is to be found in
Dugald Stewart's lectures. The great rhetorical art-critic of
our own day refers to it in words of disparagement, and in
truth it has none of the flummery of modern criticism. It
is a piece of hard thinking, and it has the distinction of
having interested and stimulated Lessing, the author of
Laoköon (1766), by far the most definitely valuable of all
the contributions to æsthetic thought in an age which was
not poor in them. Lessing was so struck with the *Inquiry* that he set about a translation of it, and the correspondence between him and Moses Mendelssohn on the
questions which Burke had raised, contains the germs of
the doctrine as to poetry and painting which *Laoköon*
afterwards made so famous. Its influence on Lessing and
on Kant was such as to justify the German historian of the
literature of the century, in bestowing on it the coveted
epithet of epoch-making.

The book is full of crudities. We feel the worse side
of the eighteenth century when Burke tells us that a
thirst for Variety in architecture is sure to leave very
little true taste ; or that an air of robustness and strength
is very prejudicial to beauty ; or that sad fuscous colours
are indispensable for sublimity. Many of the sections,
again, are little more than expanded definitions from the
dictionary. Any tiro may now be shocked at such a proposition as that beauty acts by relaxing the solids of the
whole system. But at least one signal merit remains to
the *Inquiry*. It was a vigorous enlargement of the principle,
which Addison had not long before timidly illustrated, that
critics of art seek its principles in the wrong place, so long
as they limit their search to poems, pictures, engravings,

statues, and buildings, instead of first arranging the sentiments and faculties in man to which art makes its appeal.
Addison's treatment was slight and merely literary ; Burke
dealt boldly with his subject on the base of the most
scientific psychology that was then within his reach. To
approach it on the psychological side at all, was to make
a distinct and remarkable advance in the method of the
inquiry which he had taken in hand.

CHAPTER II.

BURKE was thirty years old before he approached even the threshold of the arena in which he was destined to be so great a figure. He had made a mark in literature, and it was to literature rather than to public affairs that his ambition turned. He had naturally become acquainted with the brother authors who haunted the coffee-houses in Fleet Street; and Burke, along with his father-in-law, Dr. Nugent, was one of the first members of the immortal club where Johnson did conversational battle with all comers. We shall, in a later chapter, have something to say on Burke's friendships with the followers of his first profession, and on the active sympathy with which he helped those who were struggling into authorship. Meanwhile, the fragments that remain of his own attempts in this direction are no considerable contributions. His *Hints for an Essay on the Drama* are jejune and infertile, when compared with the vigorous and original thought of Diderot and Lessing at about the same period. He wrote an Account of the European Settlements in America. His *Abridgment of the History of England* comes down no further than to the reign of John. A much more important undertaking than his history of the past, was his design for a yearly chronicle of the present.

The *Annual Register* began to appear in 1759. Dodsley, the bookseller of Pall Mall, provided the sinews of war, and he gave Burke a hundred pounds a year for his survey of the great events which were then passing in the world. The scheme was probably born of the circumstances of the hour, for this was the climax of the Seven Years' War. The clang of arms was heard in every quarter of the globe, and in East and West new lands were being brought under the dominion of Great Britain.

In this exciting crisis of national affairs, Burke began to be acquainted with public men. In 1759 he was introduced, probably by Lord Charlemont, to William Gerard Hamilton, who only survives in our memories by his nickname of Single-speech. As a matter of fact, he made many speeches in Parliament, and some good ones, but none so good as the first, delivered in a debate in 1755, in which Pitt, Fox, Grenville, and Murray all took part, and were all outshone by the new luminary. But the new luminary never shone again with its first brilliance. He sought Burke out on the strength of the success of the *Vindication of Natural Society*, and he seems to have had a taste for good company. Horace Walpole describes a dinner at his house in the summer of 1761. " There were Garrick," he says, " and a young Mr. Burke, who wrote a book in the style of Lord Bolingbroke, that is much admired. He is a sensible man, but has not worn off his authorism yet, and thinks there is nothing so charming as writers, and to be one. He will know better one of these days." The prophecy came true in time, but it was Burke's passion for authorism that eventually led to a rupture with his first patron. Hamilton was a man of ability, but selfish and unreasonable. Dr. Leland afterwards described him compendiously as a sullen, vain, proud, selfish, canker-hearted, envious reptile.

In 1761 Hamilton went to Ireland as secretary to Lord Halifax, and Burke accompanied him in some indefinite capacity. "The absenteeism of her men of genius," an eminent historian has said, "was a worse wrong to Ireland than the absenteeism of her landlords. If Edmund Burke had remained in the country where Providence had placed him, he might have changed the current of its history."[1] It is at least to be said that Burke was never so absorbed in other affairs, as to forget the peculiar interests of his native land. We have his own word and his career does not belie it, that in the elation with which he was filled on being elected a member of Parliament, what was first and uppermost in his thoughts was the hope of being somewhat useful to the place of his birth and education ; and to the last he had in it " a dearness of instinct more than he could justify to reason." In fact the affairs of Ireland had a most important part in Burke's life at one or two critical moments, and this is as convenient a place as we are likely to find for describing in a few words what were the issues. The brief space can hardly be grudged in an account of a great political writer, for Ireland has furnished the chief ordeal, test, and standard of English statesmen.

Ireland in the middle of the eighteenth century was to England just what the American colonies would have been, if they had contained, besides the European settlers, more than twice their number of unenslaved negroes. After the suppression of the great rebellion of Tyrconnel by William of Orange, nearly the whole of the land was confiscated, the peasants were made beggars and outlaws,

2 Froude's *Ireland*, ii. 214.

the Penal Laws against the Catholics were enacted and
enforced, and the grand reign of Protestant Ascendancy
began in all its vileness and completeness.   The Protestants and landlords were supreme; the peasants and
the Catholics were prostrate in despair.   The Revolution
brought about in Ireland just the reverse of what it
effected in England.   Here it delivered the body of the
nation from the attempted supremacy of a small sect.
There it made a small sect supreme over the body of the
nation.   "It was, to say the truth," Burke wrote, "not
a revolution but a conquest," and the policy of conquest
was treated as the just and normal system of government.   The last conquest of England was in the eleventh
century.   The last conquest of Ireland was at the very end
of the seventeenth.

Sixty years after these events, when Burke revisited
Ireland, some important changes had taken place.
The English settlers of the beginning of the century
had formed an Irish interest.   They had become Anglo-
Irish, just as the colonists still further west had
formed a colonial interest and become Anglo-American.
The same conduct on the part of the mother country
promoted the growth of these hostile interests in both
cases.   The commercial policy pursued by England towards
America was identical with that pursued towards Ireland.
The industry of the Anglo-Irish traders was restricted,
their commerce and even their production fettered, their
prosperity checked, for the benefit of the merchants of
Manchester and Bristol.   *Crescit Roma Albæ ruinis.*   "The
bulk of the people," said Stone, the Primate, "are not
regularly either lodged, clothed, or fed; and those things
which in England are called necessaries of life, are to us
only accidents, and we can, and in many places do, subsist

without them." On the other hand, the peasantry had
gradually taken heart to resent their spoliation and attempted extirpation, and in 1761 their misery under the
exactions of landlords and a church which tried to spread
Christianity by the brotherly agency of the tithe-proctor,
gave birth to Whiteboyism—a terrible spectre, which,
under various names and with various modifications, has
ridden Ireland down to our own time.

Burke saw the Protestant traders of the dependency
the victims of the colonial and commercial system; the
Catholic landowners legally dispossessed by the operation
of the penal laws; the Catholic peasantry deeply
penetrated with an insurgent and vindictive spirit; and
the imperial government standing very much aloof, and
leaving the country to the tender mercies of the Under-
takers and some Protestant churchmen. The Anglo-
Irish were bitterly discontented with the mother country;
and the Catholic native Irish were regarded by their
Protestant oppressors with exactly that combination of
intense contempt and loathing, and intense rage and
terror, which their American counterpart would have
divided between the Negro and the Red Indian. To the
Anglo-Irish the native peasant was as odious as the first,
and as terrible as the second. Even at the close of the
century Burke could declare that the various descriptions
of the people were kept as much apart, as if they were
not only separate nations, but separate species. There
were thousands, he says, who had never talked to a
Roman Catholic in their whole lives, unless they happened to talk to a gardener's workman or some other
labourer of the second or third order, while a little time
before this they were so averse to have them near their
persons, that they would not employ even those who

could never find their way beyond the stables. Chesterfield, a thoroughly impartial and just observer, said in
1764 that the poor people in Ireland were used worse than
negroes by their masters and the middlemen. We should
never forget that in the transactions with the English
government during the eighteenth century, the people concerned were not the Irish, but the Anglo-Irish, the colonists
of 1691. They were an aristocracy, as Adam Smith
said of them, not founded in the natural and respectable
distinctions of birth and fortune, but in the most odious
of all distinctions, those of religious and political prejudices—distinctions which, more than any other, animate
both the insolence of the oppressors, and the hatred and
indignation of the oppressed.

The directions in which Irish improvement would
move, were clear from the middle of the century to men
with much less foresight than Burke had. The removal
of all commercial restrictions, either by Independence or
Union, on the one hand ; and the gradual emancipation
of the Catholics, on the other ; were the two processes to
which every consideration of good government manifestly
pointed. The first proved a much shorter and simpler
process than the second. To the first the only obstacle was
the blindness and selfishness of the English merchants.
The second had to overcome the virulent opposition of the
tyrannical Protestant faction in Ireland, and the disgrace-
ful but deep-rooted antipathies of the English nation.
The history of the relation between the mother country and
her dependency during Burke's life, may be characterized as
a commercial and legislative struggle between the imperial
government and the Anglo-Irish interest, in which each
side for its own convenience, as the turn served, drew
support from the Catholic majority.

A Whiteboy outbreak, attended by the usual circumstances of disorder and violence, took place while Burke
was in Ireland. It suited the interests of faction to represent these commotions as the symptoms of a deliberate
rebellion. The malcontents were represented as carrying
on treasonable correspondence, sometimes with Spain and
sometimes with France ; they were accused of receiving
money and arms from their foreign sympathizers, and of
aiming at throwing off the English rule. Burke says that
he had means and the desire of informing himself to the
bottom upon the matter, and he came strongly to the conclusion that this was not a true view of what had happened.
What had happened was due, he thought, to no plot, but
to superficial and fortuitous circumstances. He conse-
quently did not shrink from describing it as criminal,
that the king's Catholic subjects in Ireland should have
been subjected, on no good grounds, to harassing persecution, and that numbers of them should have been ruined
in fortune, imprisoned, tried, and capitally executed for a
rebellion which was no rebellion at all. The episode is
only important as illustrating the strong and manly temper
in which Burke, unlike too many of his countrymen with
fortunes to make by English favour, uniformly considered
the circumstances of his country. It was not until a
later time that he had an opportunity of acting con-
spicuously on her behalf, but whatever influence he came
to acquire with his party was unflinchingly used against
the cruelty of English prejudice.

Burke appears to have remained in Ireland for two
years (1761-3). In 1763 Hamilton, who had found
him an invaluable auxiliary, procured for him, principally
with the aid of the Primate Stone, a pension of three hundred pounds a year from the Irish Treasury. In thanking

him for this service, Burke proceeded to bargain that the
obligation should not bind him to give to his patron the
whole of his time. He insisted on being left with a dis-
creet liberty to continue a little work which he had as a
rent-charge upon his thoughts. Whatever advantages he
had acquired, he says, had been due to literary reputation,
and he could only hope for a continuance of such advantages on condition of doing something to keep the same
reputation alive. What this literary design was, we do
not know with certainty. It is believed to have been a
history of England, of which, as I have said, a fragment
remains. Whatever the work may have been, it was an
offence to Hamilton. With an irrational stubbornness,
that may well astound us when we think of the noble
genius that he thus wished to confine to paltry personal
duties, he persisted that Burke should bind himself to his
service for life, and to the exclusion of other interests. " To
circumscribe my hopes," cried Burke, " to give up even the
possibility of liberty, to annihilate myself for ever ! " He
threw up the pension, which he had held for two years,
and declined all further connexion with Hamilton, whom
he roundly described as an infamous scoundrel. " Six of
the best years of my life he took me from every pursuit of
my literary reputation, or of improvement of my fortune. . . .
In all this time you may easily conceive how much I felt
at seeing myself left behind by almost all of my contemporaries. There never was a season more favourable for
any man who chose to enter into the career of public life ;
and I think I am not guilty of ostentation in supposing
my own moral character, and my industry, my friends and
connexions, when Mr. Hamilton first sought my acquaintance, were not at all inferior to those of several whose fortune is at this day upon a very different footing from mine."

It was not long before a more important opening offered
itself, which speedily brought Burke into the main stream
of public life. In the summer of 1765 a change of ministry
took place. It was the third since the king's accession
five years ago. First, Pitt had been disgraced, and the old
Duke of Newcastle dismissed. Then Bute came into power,
but Bute quailed before the storm of calumny and hate
which his Scotch nationality, and the supposed source of his
power over the king, had raised in every town in England.
After Lord Bute, George Grenville undertook the Government.   Before he had been many months in office, he had
sown the seeds of war in the colonies, wearied parliament,
and disgusted the king.   In June, 1765, Grenville was
dismissed. With profound reluctance the king had no other
choice than to summon Lord Rockingham, and Lord Rockingham, in a happy moment for himself and his party,
was induced to offer Burke a post as his private secretary.
A government by country gentlemen is too apt to be a
government of ignorance, and Lord Rockingham was
without either experience or knowledge. He felt, or friends
felt for him, the advantage of having at his side a man who
was chiefly known as an author in the service of Dodsley,
and as having conducted the *Annual Register* with great
ability, but who even then was widely spoken of as
nothing less than an encyclopædia of political knowledge.

It is commonly believed that Burke was commended to
Lord Rockingham by William Fitzherbert. Fitzherbert
was President of the Board of Trade in the new government, but he is more likely to be remembered as Dr.
Johnson's famous example of the truth of the observation,
that a man will please more upon the whole by negative
qualities than by positive, because he was the most

acceptable man in London, and yet overpowered nobody
by the superiority of his talents, made no man think
worse of himself by being his rival, seemed always to
listen, did not oblige you to hear much from him, and
did not oppose what you said.   Besides Fitzherbert's influence, we have it on Burke's own authority that his
promotion was partly due to that mysterious person,
William Burke, who was at the same time appointed
an under-secretary of state.   There must have been unpleasant rumours afloat as to the Burke connexion, and
we shall presently consider what they were worth.
Meanwhile, it is enough to say that the old Duke of
Newcastle hurried to the new premier, and told him the
appointment would never do : that the new secretary was
not only an Irish adventurer, which was true, but that
he was an Irish papist, which was not true ; that he was a
Jesuit, that he was a spy from Saint Omer's, and that his
real name was O'Bourke.   Lord Rockingham behaved like a
man of sense and honour, sent for Burke, and repeated to
him what he had heard.   Burke warmly denounced the
truthlessness of the Duke's tattle : he insisted that the
reports which his chief had heard would probably, even
unknown to himself, create in his mind such suspicions as
would stand in the way of a thorough confidence.   No
earthly consideration, he said, should induce him to
continue in relations with a man whose trust in him was
not entire ; and he pressed his resignation.   To this
Lord Rockingham would not consent, and from that time
until his death, seventeen years afterwards, the relations between them were those of loyal and honourable
service on the one hand, and generous and appreciative
friendship on the other.   Six-and-twenty years afterwards
(1791) Burke remembered the month, in which he had

first become connected with a man whose memory, he
said, will ever be precious to Englishmen of all parties,
as long as the ideas of honour and virtue, public and
private, are understood and cherished in this nation.

The Rockingham ministry remained in office for a year
and twenty days (1765-6). About the middle of this
term (Dec. 26, 1765), Burke was returned to Parliament
for the borough of Wendover, by the influence of Lord
Verney, who owned it, and who also returned William
Burke for another borough. Lord Verney was an Irish
peer, with large property in Buckinghamshire; he now
represented that county in parliament. It was William
Burke's influence with Lord Verney that procured for his
namesake the seat at Wendover. Burke made his first
speech in the House of Commons a few days after the
opening of the session of 1766 (Jan. 27), and was honoured
by a compliment from Pitt, still the Great Commoner. A
week later he spoke again on the same momentous theme,
the complaints of the American colonists, and his success
was so marked that good judges predicted, in the stiff
phraseology of the time, that he would soon add the palm
of the orator to the laurel of the writer and the philosopher. The friendly Dr. Johnson wrote to Langton, that
Burke had gained more reputation than any man at his
first appearance had ever gained before. The session was
a great triumph to the new member, but it brought
neither strength nor popularity to the administration.
At the end of it, the king dismissed them, and the
Chatham government was formed; that strange combination which has been made famous by Burke's description
of it, as a piece of joinery so crossly indented and whimsically dove-tailed, such a piece of diversified mosaic, such a
tesselated pavement without cement, that it was indeed a

very curious show, but utterly unsafe to touch and un-
sure to stand upon. There was no obvious reason why
Burke should not have joined the new ministry. The
change was at first one of persons, rather than of principles
or of measures. To put himself, as Burke afterwards
said, out of the way of the negotiations which were then
being carried on very eagerly and through many channels
with the Earl of Chatham, he went to Ireland very soon
after the change of ministry. He was free from party
engagements, and more than this, he was free at the express desire of his friends; for on the very day of his return,
the Marquis of Rockingham wished him to accept office
under the new system. Burke "believes he might have
had such a situation, but he cheerfully took his fate with
his party." In a short time he rendered his party the
first of a long series of splendid literary services by writing
his *Observations on the Present State of the Nation* (1769).
It was a reply to a pamphlet by George Grenville, in
which the disappointed minister accused his successors of
ruining the country. Burke, in answering the charge,
showed a grasp of commercial and fiscal details at least
equal to that of Grenville himself, then considered the
first man of his time in dealing with the national trade
and resources. To this easy mastery of the special facts
of the discussion, Burke added the far rarer art of lighting
them up by broad principles, and placing himself and his
readers at the highest and most effective point of view for
commanding their general bearings.

If Burke had been the Irish adventurer that his enemies
described, he might well have seized with impatience the
opening to office, that the recent exhibition of his powers
in the House of Commons had now made accessible to
him. There was not a man in Great Britain to whom the

emoluments of office would have been more useful. It is
one of the standing mysteries in literary biography, how
Burke could think of entering Parliament without any
means that anybody can now trace of earning a fitting
livelihood. Yet at this time Burke, whom we saw not
long ago writing for the booksellers, had become affluent
enough to pay a yearly allowance to Barry, the painter,
in order to enable him to study the pictures in the great
European galleries, and to make a prolonged residence at
Rome. A little later he took a step which makes the
riddle still more difficult, and which has given abundant
employment to wits who are *maximi in minimis*, and
think that every question which they can ask, yet to
which history has thought it worth while to leave no
answer, is somehow a triumph of their own learning and
dialectic.

In 1769 Burke purchased a house and lands known as
Gregories, in the parishes of Penn and Beaconsfield, in the
county of Bucks. It has often been asked, and naturally
enough, how a man who, hardly more than a few months
before, was still contented to earn an extra hundred pounds
a year by writing for Dodsley, should now have launched
out as the buyer of a fine house and estate, which cost
upwards of twenty-two thousand pounds, which could not
be kept up on less than two thousand five hundred a year,
and of which the returns did not amount to one-fifth of
that sum. Whence did he procure the money, and what
is perhaps more difficult to answer, how came he first to
entertain the idea of a design so ill-proportioned to anything that we can now discern in his means and prospects? The common answer from Burke's enemies, and
even from some neutral inquirers, gives to every lover of
this great man's high character an unpleasant shock. It

is alleged that he had plunged into furious gambling in East India stock. The charge was current at the time, and it was speedily revived when Burke's abandonment of his party, after the French Revolution, exposed him to a thousand attacks of reckless and uncontrolled virulence. It has been stirred by one or two pertinacious critics nearer our own time, and none of the biographers have dealt with the perplexities of the matter as they ought to have done. Nobody, indeed, has ever pretended to find one jot or tittle of direct evidence that Burke himself took a part in the gambling in India or other stocks. There is evidence that he was a holder of the stock, and no more. But what is undeniable is that Richard Burke, his brother, William Burke, his intimate if not his kinsman, and Lord Verney, his political patron, were all three at this time engaged together in immense transactions in East India stock ; that in 1769 the stock fell violently ; that they were unable to pay their differences ; and that in the very year in which Edmund Burke bought Gregories, they were utterly ruined, two of them beyond retrieval. Again it is clear that, after this, Richard Burke was engaged in land-jobbing in the West Indies ; that his claims were disputed by the Government as questionable and dishonest ; and that he lost his case. Edmund Burke was said, in the gossip of the day, to be deeply interested in land at Saint Vincent's. But there is no evidence. What cannot be denied is that an unpleasant taint of speculation and financial adventurership hung at one time about the whole connexion, and that the adventures invariably came to an unlucky end.

Whether Edmund Burke and William Burke were relations or not, and if so, in what degree they were relations, neither of them ever knew ; they believed that

their fathers sometimes called one another cousins, and
that was all that they had to say on the subject. But
they were as intimate as brothers, and when William
Burke went to mend his broken fortunes in India, Edmund Burke commended him to Philip Francis,—then
fighting his deadly duel of five years with Warren
Hastings at Calcutta—as one whom he had tenderly loved,
highly valued, and continually lived with in an union
not to be expressed, quite since their boyish years. "Looking back to the course of my life," he wrote in 1771, "I
remember no one considerable benefit in the whole of it
which I did not, mediately or immediately, derive from
William Burke." There is nothing intrinsically incredible,
therefore, considering this intimacy and the community
of purse and home which subsisted among the three
Burkes, in the theory that when Edmund Burke bought
his property in Buckinghamshire, he looked for help from
the speculations of Richard and William. However this
may have been, from them no help came. Many years
afterwards (1783), Lord Verney filed a bill in Chancery
claiming from Edmund Burke a sum of 6000*l.*, which he
alleged that he had lent at the instigation of William
Burke to assist in completing the purchase of Beaconsfield. Burke's sworn answer denied all knowledge of the
transaction, and the plaintiff did not get the relief for
which he had prayed.

In a letter to Shackleton (May 1, 1768,) Burke gave
the following account of what he had done :—" I have
made a push," he says, " with all I could collect of my
own, and the aid of my friends, to cast a little root in this
country. I have purchased a house, with an estate of
about six hundred acres of land, in Buckinghamshire,
twenty-four miles from London. It is a place exceedingly

pleasant; and I propose, God willing, to become a farmer in good earnest. You who are classical will not be displeased to know that it was formerly the seat of Waller, the poet, whose house, or part of it, makes at present the farm-house within an hundred yards of me." The details of the actual purchase of Beaconsfield have been made tolerably clear. The price was twenty-two thousand pounds, more or less. Fourteen thousand were left on mortgage, which remained outstanding until the sale of the property by Mrs. Burke in 1812. Garret Burke, the elder brother, had shortly before the purchase made Edmund his residuary legatee, and this bequest is rather conjecturally estimated at two thousand pounds. The balance of six thousand was advanced by Lord Rockingham on Burke's bond.

The purchase after all was the smallest part of the matter, and it still remains a puzzle not only how Burke was able to maintain so handsome an establishment, but how he could ever suppose it likely that he would be able to maintain it. He counted, no doubt, on making some sort of income by farming, but then he might well have known that an absorbed politician would hardly be able, as he called it, to turn farmer in good earnest. For a short time he received a salary of seven hundred pounds a year as agent for New York. We may perhaps take for granted that he made as much more out of his acres. He received something from Dodsley for his work on the *Annual Register* down to 1788. But when all these resources have been counted up, we cannot but see the gulf of a great yearly deficit. The unhappy truth is that from the middle of 1769, when we find him applying to Garrick for the loan of a thousand pounds, down to 1794 when the king gave him a pension, Burke was never free from the harassing strain of debts and want of money. It has been stated with good show of authority, that his obligations to Lord Rockingham amounted to not less than thirty thousand pounds. When that nobleman died (1782), with a generosity which is not the less honourable to him for having been so richly earned by the faithful friend who was the object of it, he left instructions to his executors that all Burke's bonds should be destroyed.

We may indeed wish from the bottom of our hearts that all this had been otherwise. But those who press it as a reproach against Burke's memory, may be justly reminded that when Pitt died, after drawing the pay of a minister for twenty years, he left debts to the amount of forty thousand pounds. Burke, as I have said elsewhere, had none of the vices of profusion, but he had that quality which Aristotle places high among the virtues—the noble mean of Magnificence, standing midway between the two extremes of vulgar ostentation and narrow pettiness. At least, every creditor was paid in good time, and nobody suffered but himself. Those who think these disagreeable matters of supreme importance, and allow such things to stand between them and Burke's greatness, are like the people—slightly to alter a figure from a philosopher of old—who, when they went to Olympia, could only perceive that they were scorched by the sun, and pressed by the crowd, and deprived of comfortable means of bathing, and wetted by the rain, and that life was full of disagreeable and troublesome things, and so they almost forgot the great colossus of ivory and gold, Phidias's statue of Zeus, which they had come to see, and which stood in all its glory and power before their perturbed and foolish vision.

There have been few men in history with whom per-

sonal objects counted for so little as they counted with
Burke. He really did what so many public men only
feign to do. He forgot that he had any interests of his
own to be promoted, apart from the interests of the
party with which he acted, and from those of the whole
nation, for which he held himself a trustee. What
William Burke said of him in 1766, was true throughout his life,—"Ned is full of real business, intent
upon doing solid good to his country, as much as if
he was to receive twenty per cent. from the Empire."
Such men as the shrewd and impudent Rigby atoned
for a plebeian origin by the arts of dependence and a
judicious servility, and drew more of the public money
from the pay office in half-a-dozen quarter-days, than
Burke received in all his life. It was not by such arts
that Burke rose. When we remember all the untold
bitterness of the struggle in which he was engaged, from
the time when the old Duke of Newcastle tried to make
the Marquis of Rockingham dismiss his new private secretary as an Irish Jesuit in disguise (1765), down to the
time when the Duke of Bedford, himself battening "in
grants to the house of Russell, so enormous as not only to
outrage economy, but even to stagger credibility," assailed
the government for giving Burke a moderate pension, we
may almost imagine that if Johnson had imitated the
famous Tenth Satire a little later, he would have been
tempted to apply the poet's cynical criticism of the career
heroic, to the greater Cicero of his own day. " I was not,"
Burke said, in a passage of lofty dignity, "like his Grace
of Bedford, swaddled and rocked and dandled into a
legislator ; *Nitor in adversum* is the motto for a man like
me. I possessed not one of the qualities, nor cultivated
one of the arts, that recommend men to the favour and pro-

tection of the great. I was not made for a minion or a
tool.   As little did I follow the trade of winning the
hearts, by imposing on the understandings of the people.
At every step of my progress in life, for in every step was
I traversed and opposed, and at every turnpike I met, I
was obliged to show my passport, and again and again to
prove my sole title to the honour of being useful to my
country, by a proof that I was not wholly unacquainted
with its laws and the whole system of its interests both
abroad and at home ; otherwise no rank, no toleration
even for me."

CHAPTER III.

FOREIGN observers of our affairs looked upon the state of England between the accession of George III., and the loss of the American colonies (1760—1776), with mixed disgust and satisfaction. Their instinct as absolute rulers was revolted by a spectacle of unbridled faction and raging anarchy; their envy was soothed by the growing weakness of a power which Chatham had so short a time before left at the highest point of grandeur and strength. Frederick the Great spoke with contempt of the insolence of Opposition and the virulence of parties; and vowed that, petty German prince as he was, he would not change places with the King of England. The Emperor Joseph pronounced positively that Great Britain was declining, that Parliament was ruining itself, and that the colonies threatened a catastrophe. Catherine of Russia thought that nothing would restore its ancient vigour to the realm, short of the bracing and heroic remedy of a war. Even at home, such shrewd and experienced onlookers as Horace Walpole suspected that the state of the country was more serious than it had been since the Great Rebellion, and declared it to be approaching by fast strides to some sharp crisis. Men who remembered their Roman history, fancied that they saw every symptom of confusion that preceded

the ruin of the Commonwealth, and began to inquire
uneasily what was the temper of the army.   Men who
remembered the story of the violence and insatiable factiousness of Florence, turned again to Macchiavelli and to
Guicciardini, to trace a parallel between the fierce city on
the Arno and the fierce city on the Thames.   When the
King of Sweden, in 1772, carried out a revolution, by
abolishing an oligarchic council and assuming the powers
of a dictator, with the assent of his people, there were
actually serious men in England who thought that the
English, after having been guilty of every meanness and
corruption, would soon, like the Swedes, own themselves
unworthy to be free.   The Duke of Richmond, who happened to have a claim to a peerage and an estate in France,
excused himself for taking so much pains to establish his
claim to them, by gravely asking who knew that a time
might not soon come when England would not be worthy
living in, and when a retreat to France might be a very
happy thing for a free man to have ?

   The reign had begun by a furious outbreak of hatred
between the English and the Scotch.   Lord Bute had
been driven from office, not merely because he was supposed to owe his power to a scandalous friendship with
the King's mother, but because he was accused of crowding
the public service with his detested countrymen from the
other side of the Tweed.   He fell, less from disapproval of
his policy, than from rude prejudice against his country.
The flow of angry emotion had not subsided before the
whisper of strife in the American colonies began to trouble
the air ; and before that had waxed loud, the Middlesex
election had blown into a portentous hurricane.   This
was the first great constitutional case after Burke came
into the House of Commons.   As, moreover, it became a

leading element in the crisis which was the occasion of Burke's first remarkable essay in the literature of politics, it is as well to go over the facts.

The Parliament to which he had first been returned, now approaching the expiry of its legal term, was dissolved in the spring of 1768. Wilkes, then an outlaw in Paris, returned to England, and announced himself as a candidate for the City. When the election was over, his name stood last on the poll. But his ancient fame as the opponent and victim of the court five years before, were revived. After his rejection in the City, he found himself strong enough to stand for the county of Middlesex. Here he was returned at the head of the poll after an excited election. Wilkes had been tried in 1764, and found guilty by the King's Bench of republishing Number Forty-five of the *North Briton,* and of printing and publishing the *Essay on Woman.* He had not appeared to receive sentence, and had been outlawed in consequence. After his election for Middlesex, he obtained a reversal of his outlawry on a point of technical form. He then came up for sentence under the original verdict. The court sent him to prison for twenty-two months, and condemned him to pay a fine of a thousand pounds.

Wilkes was in prison when the second session of the new Parliament began. His case came before the House in November, 1768, on his own petition, accusing Lord Mansfield of altering the record at his trial. After many acrimonious debates and examinations of Wilkes and others at the bar of the House, at length, by 219 votes against 136, the famous motion was passed which expelled him from the House. Another election for Middlesex was now held, and Wilkes was returned without opposition. The day after the return, the House of Commons

resolved by an immense majority, that having been expelled, Wilkes was incapable of serving in that Parliament.   The following month Wilkes was once more
elected.   The House once more declared the election void.
In April another election took place, and this time the
Government put forward Colonel Luttrell, who vacated his
seat for Bossiney for the purpose of opposing Wilkes.
There was the same result, and for the fourth time Wilkes
was at the head of the poll.   The House ordered the
return to be altered, and after hearing by counsel the
freeholders of Middlesex who petitioned against the alteration, finally confirmed it (May 8, 1769) by a majority of
221 to 152.   According to Lord Temple, this was the
greatest majority ever known on the last day of a session.

The purport and significance of these arbitrary proceedings need little interpretation.   The House, according to
the authorities, had a constitutional right to expel Wilkes,
though the grounds on which even this is defended, would
probably be questioned if a similar case were to arise in
our own day.   But a single branch of the legislature could
have no power to pass an incapacitating vote either against
Wilkes or anybody else.   An Act of Parliament is the
least instrument by which such incapacity could be imposed.   The House might perhaps expel Wilkes, but it
could not either legally or with regard to the less definite
limits of constitutional morality, decide whom the Middlesex freeholders should not elect, and it could not therefore set aside their representative, who was then free from
any disabling quality.   Lord Camden did not much exag-
gerate, when he declared in a debate on the subject in
the House of Lords, that the judgment passed upon the
Middlesex election had given the constitution a more dangerous wound, than any which were given during the twelve

years' absence of Parliament in the reign of Charles I. The House of Commons was usurping another form of that very dispensing power, for pretending to which the last of the Stuart sovereigns had lost his crown. If the House by a vote could deprive Wilkes of a right to sit, what legal or constitutional impediment would there be in the way, if the majority were at any time disposed to declare all their most formidable opponents in the minority incapable of sitting?

In the same Parliament, there was another and scarcely less remarkable case of Privilege, "that eldest son of Prerogative," as Burke truly called it, "and inheriting all the vices of its parent." Certain printers were accused of breach of privilege for reporting the debates of the House (March, 1771). The messenger of the serjeant-at-arms attempted to take one of them into custody in his own shop in the City. A constable was standing by, designedly, it has been supposed, and Miller, the printer, gave the messenger into his custody for an assault. The case came on before the Lord Mayor, Alderman Wilkes, and Alderman Oliver, the same evening, and the result was that the messenger of the House was committed. The City doctrine was, that if the House of Commons had a serjeant-at-arms, they had a serjeant-at-mace. If the House of Commons could send their citizens to Newgate, they could send its messenger to the Compter. Two other printers were collusively arrested, brought before Wilkes and Oliver, and at once liberated.

The Commons instantly resolved on stern measures. The Lord Mayor and Oliver were taken and dispatched to the Tower, where they lay until the prorogation of Parliament. Wilkes stubbornly refused to pay any attention to repeated summonses to attend at the bar of the

House, very properly insisting that he ought to be summoned to attend *in his place* as member for Middlesex. Besides committing Crosby and Oliver to the Tower, the House summoned the Lord Mayor's clerk to attend with his books, and then and there forced him to strike out the record of the recognisances into which their messenger had entered on being committed at the Mansion House. No Stuart ever did anything more arbitrary and illegal. The House deliberately intended to constitute itself, as Burke had said two years before, an arbitrary and despotic assembly. The distempers of monarchy were the great subjects of apprehension and redress in the last century. In this, the distempers of Parliament."

Burke, in a speech which he delivered in his place in 1771, warned the House of the evils of the course upon which they were entering, and declared those to be their mortal enemies who would persuade them to act as if they were a self-originated magistracy, independent of the people, and unconnected with their opinions and feelings. But these mortal enemies of its very constitution were at this time the majority of the House. It was to no purpose that Burke argued with more than legal closeness that incapacitation could not be a power according to law, inasmuch as it had neither of the two properties of law : it was not *known*, "you yourselves not knowing upon what grounds you will vote the incapacity of any man ; " and it was not *fixed*, because it was varied according to the occasion, exercised according to discretion, and no man could call for it as a right. A strain of unanswerable reasoning of this kind counted for nothing, in spite of its being unanswerable. Despotic or oligarchic pretensions are proof against the most formidable battery that reason and experience can construct against them. And Wilkes's

exclusion endured until this Parliament—the Unreported
Parliament, as it was called, and in many respects the
very worst that ever assembled at Westminster—was
dissolved, and a new one elected (1774), when he was
once again returned for Middlesex, and took his seat.

The London multitude had grown zealous for Wilkes,
and the town had been harassed by disorder. Of the fierce
brutality of the crowd of that age, we may form a vivid
idea from the unflinching pencil of Hogarth. Barbarous
laws were cruelly administered. The common people
were turbulent, because misrule made them miserable.
Wilkes had written filthy verses, but the crowd cared no
more for this than their betters cared about the vices of
Lord Sandwich. They made common cause with one who
was accidentally a more conspicuous sufferer. Wilkes was
quite right when he vowed that he was no Wilkite. The
masses were better than their leader. "Whenever the
people have a feeling," Burke once said, "they commonly
are in the right: they sometimes mistake the physician."
Franklin, who was then in London, was of opinion that
if George III. had had a bad character, and John Wilkes
a good one, the latter might have turned the former out
of the kingdom; for the turbulence that began in street
riots, at one time threatened to end in revolt. The king
himself was attacked with savage invective in papers of
which it was said, that no one in the previous century
would have dared to print any like them until Charles
was fast locked up in Carisbrooke Castle.

As is usual when the minds of those in power have
been infected with an arbitrary temper, the employment
of military force to crush civil disturbances became a
familiar and favourite idea. The military, said Lord Wey-
mouth, in an elaborate letter which he addressed to the

Surrey magistrates, can never be employed to a more constitutional purpose than in the support of the authority and
dignity of the magistracy.   If the magistrate should be
menaced, he is cautioned not to delay a moment in calling
for the aid of the military, and making use of them effectually.   The consequence of this bloody scroll, as Wilkes
rightly called it, was that shortly afterwards an affray
occurred between the crowd and the troops, in which
some twenty people were killed and wounded (May 10,
1768).   On the following day, the Secretary of War, Lord
Barrington, wrote to the commanding officer, informing
him that the King highly approved of the conduct both
of officers and men, and wished that his gracious appro-
bation of them should be communicated to them.

Burke brought the matter before the House in a motion
for a Committee of Inquiry, supported by one of the
most lucid and able of his minor speeches.   "If ever
the time should come," he concluded, " when this House
shall be found prompt to execute and slow to inquire ;
ready to punish the excesses of the people, and slow to
listen to their grievances ; ready to grant supplies, and
slow to examine the account ; ready to invest magistrates
with large powers, and slow to inquire into the exercise of
them ; ready to entertain notions of the military power as
incorporated with the constitution,—when you learn this
in the air of St. James's, then the business is done ; then
the House of Commons will change that character which
it receives from the people only."   It is hardly necessary
to say that his motion for a committee was lost by the
overwhelming majority of two hundred and forty-five
against thirty.   The general result of the proceedings of the
government from the accession of George III. to the beginning of the troubles in the American colonies, was in Burke's

own words, that the government was at once dreaded and contemned; that the laws were despoiled of all their respected and salutary terrors; that their inaction was a subject of ridicule, and their exertion of abhorrence; that our dependencies had slackened in their affections; that we knew neither how to yield, nor how to enforce; and that disconnexion and confusion, in offices, in parties, in families, in parliament, in the nation, prevailed beyond the disorders of any former time.

It was in the pamphlet on the *Present Discontents*, published in 1770, that Burke dealt at large with the whole scheme of policy of which all these irregularities were the distempered incidents. The pamphlet was composed as a manifesto of the Rockingham section of the Whig party, to show, as Burke wrote to his chief, how different it was in spirit and composition from " the Bedfords, the Grenvilles, and other knots, who are combined for no public purpose, but only as a means of furthering with joint strength their private and individual advantage." The pamphlet was submitted in manuscript or proof to the heads of the party. Friendly critics excused some inelegancies which they thought they found in occasional passages, by taking for granted, as was true, that he had admitted insertions from other hands. Here for the first time he exhibited, on a conspicuous scale, the strongest qualities of his under-standing. Contemporaries had an opportunity of measuring this strength, by comparison with another performance of similar scope. The letters of Junius had startled the world the year before. Burke was universally suspected of being their author, and the suspicion never wholly died out so long as he lived. There was no real ground for it beyond the two unconnected facts, that the letters were powerful letters, and that Burke had a powerful

intellect.   Dr. Johnson admitted that he had never had a
better reason for believing that Burke was Junius, than
that he knew nobody else who had the ability of Junius.
But Johnson discharged his mind of the thought, at the
instant that Burke voluntarily assured him that he neither
wrote the letters of Junius, nor knew who had written
them.   The subjects and aim of those famous pieces were
not very different from Burke's tract, but any one who in
our time turns from the letters to the tract, will wonder how
the author of the one could ever have been suspected of
writing the other.   Junius is never more than a railer,
and very often he is third-rate even as a railer.   The author
of the *Present Discontents* speaks without bitterness even
of Lord Bute and the Duke of Grafton ; he only refers to
persons, when their conduct or their situation illustrates a
principle.   Instead of reviling, he probes, he reflects, he
warns ; and as the result of this serious method, pursued
by a man in whom close mastery of detail kept exact pace
with wide grasp of generalities, we have not the epheme-
ral diatribe of a faction, but one of the monumental pieces
of political literature.

The last great pamphlet in the history of English
public affairs had been Swift's tract *On the Conduct of
the Allies* (1711), in which the writer did a more substantial service for the Tory party of his day, than Burke
did for the Whig party of a later date.   Swift's pamphlet
is close, strenuous, persuasive, and full of telling strokes ;
but nobody need read it to-day, except the historical
student, or a member of the Peace Society, in search
of the most convincing exposure of the most insane
of English wars.[1]   There is not a sentence in it which

[1] This was not Burke's judgment on the long war against
Louis XIV.   See *Regicide Peace*, i.

does not belong exclusively to the matter in hand : not a line of that general wisdom which is for all time. In the *Present Discontents* the method is just the opposite of this. The details are slurred, and they are not literal. Burke describes with excess of elaboration how the new system is a system of double cabinets ; one put forward with nominal powers in Parliament, the other concealed behind the throne, and secretly dictating the policy. The reader feels that this is worked out far too closely to be real. It is a structure of artificial rhetoric. But we lightly pass this over, on our way to more solid matter ; to the exposition of the principles of a constitution, the right methods of statesmanship, and the defence of party.

It was Bolingbroke, and not Swift, of whom Burke was thinking, when he sat down to the composition of his tract. The *Patriot King* was the fountain of the new doctrines, which Burke trained his party to understand and to resist. If his foe was domestic, it was from a foreign armoury that Burke derived the instruments of resistance. The great fault of political writers is their too close adherence to the forms of the system of state which they happen to be expounding or examining. They stop short at the anatomy of institutions, and do not penetrate to the secret of their functions. An illustrious author in the middle of the eighteenth century introduced his contemporaries to a better way. It is not too much to say that at that epoch the strength of political speculation in this country, from Adam Smith downwards, was drawn from France ; and Burke had been led to some of what was most characteristic in his philosophy of society by Montesquieu's *Spirit of Laws* (1748), the first great manual of the historic school. We have no space here to work out the relations between Montesquieu's principles

E

and Burke's, but the student of the *Esprit des Lois* will recognize its influence in every one of Burke's masterpieces.

So far as immediate events were concerned, Burke was quick to discern their true interpretation. As has been already said, he attributed to the King and his party a deliberateness of system which probably had no real existence in their minds. The King intended to reassert the old right of choosing his own ministers. George II. had made strenuous but futile endeavours to the same end. His son, the father of George III., Frederick, Prince of Wales, as every reader of Dodington's Diary will remember, was equally bent on throwing off the yoke of the great Whig combinations, and making his own cabinets. George III. was only continuing the purpose of his father and his grandfather; and there is no reason to believe that he went more elaborately to work to obtain his ends.

It is when he leaves the artifices of a cabal, and strikes down below the surface to the working of deep social forces, that we feel the breadth and power of Burke's method. "I am not one of those," he began, "who think that the people are never wrong. They have been so, frequently and outrageously, both in other countries and in this. But I do say that *in all disputes between them and their rulers, the presumption is at least upon a par in favour of the people.*" Nay, experience perhaps justifies him in going further. When popular discontents are prevalent, something has generally been found amiss in the constitution or the administration. " The people have no interest in disorder. When they go wrong, it is their error, and not their crime." And then he quotes the famous passage from the Memoirs of Sully, which both

practical politicians and political students should bind
about their necks, and write upon the tables of their
hearts :—" The revolutions that come to pass in great states
are not the result of chance, nor of popular caprice. . . . .
As for the populace, it is never from a passion for attack
that it rebels, but from impatience of suffering."
What really gives its distinction to the *Present Discontents* is not its plea for indulgence to popular impatience, nor its plea for the superiority of government by
aristocracy, but rather the presence in it of the thought
of Montesquieu and his school, of the necessity of studying
political phenomena in relation, not merely to forms of
government and law, but in relation to whole groups of
social facts which give to law and government the spirit
that makes them workable. Connected with this, is a
particularly wide interpretation and a particularly impressive application of the maxims of expediency, because
a wide conception of the various interacting elements of a
society naturally extends the considerations which a
balance of expediencies will include. Hence, in time,
there came a strong and lofty ideal of the true statesman,
his breadth of vision, his flexibility of temper, his hardly
measurable influence. These are the principal thoughts
in the *Discontents* to which that tract owes its permanent
interest. " Whatever original energy," says Burke, in one
place, " may be supposed either in force or regulation, the
operation of both is in truth merely instrumental. Nations
are governed by the same methods, and on the same principles, by which an individual without authority is often able
to govern those who are his equals or superiors; by a knowledge of their temper, and by a judicious management of
it. . . . . The laws reach but a very little way. Constitute Government how you please, infinitely the greater

E 2

part of it must depend upon the exercise of powers, which
are left at large to the prudence and uprightness of ministers of state. Even all the use and potency of the laws
depends upon them. Without them, your Commonwealth
is no better than *a scheme upon paper ; and not a living,
active, effective constitution.*" Thus early in his public
career had Burke seized that great antithesis which he so
eloquently laboured in the long and ever memorable episode
of his war against the French Revolution : the opposition
between artificial arrangements in politics, and a living,
active, effective organization, formed by what he calls elsewhere in the present tract, the natural strength of the
kingdom, and suitable to the temper and mental habits of
the people. When he spoke of the natural strength of
the kingdom, he gave no narrow or conventional account
of it. He included in the elements of that strength, besides the great peers and the leading landed gentlemen,
the opulent merchants and manufacturers, and the substantial yeomanry. Contrasted with the trite versions of
government as fixed in King, Lords, and Commons, this
search for the real organs of power was going to the root
of the matter in a spirit at once thoroughly scientific and
thoroughly practical. Burke had, by the speculative
training to which he had submitted himself in dealing
with Bolingbroke, prepared his mind for a complete grasp
of the idea of the body politic as a complex growth, a
manifold whole, with closely interdependent relations
among its several parts and divisions. It was this conception from which his conservatism sprang. Revolutionary
politics have one of their sources in the idea that societies
are capable of infinite and immediate modifications,
without reference to the deep-rooted conditions that have
worked themselves into every part of the social structure.

The same opposition of the positive to the doctrinaire
spirit is to be observed in the remarkable vindication of
Party, which fills the last dozen pages of the pamphlet,
and which is one of the most courageous of all Burke's
deliverances. Party combination is exactly one of those
contrivances which, as it might seem, a wise man would
accept for working purposes, but about which he would
take care to say as little as possible. There appears to be
something revolting to the intellectual integrity and self-
respect of the individual, in the systematic surrender of his
personal action, interest, and power, to a political connexion in which his own judgment may never once be
allowed to count for anything. It is like the surrender
of the right of private judgment to the authority of the
Church, but with its nakedness not concealed by a mystic
doctrine. Nothing is more easy to demolish by the bare
logical reason. But Burke cared nothing about the bare
logical reason, until it had been clothed in convenience
and custom, in the affections on one side, and experience
on the other. Not content with insisting that for some
special purpose of the hour, " when bad men combine, the
good must associate," he contended boldly for the merits of
fidelity to party combination in itself. Although Burke
wrote these strong pages as a reply to Bolingbroke, who
had denounced party as an evil, they remain as the best
general apology that has ever been offered for that principle of public action, against more philosophic attacks
than Bolingbroke's. Burke admitted that when he saw a
man acting a desultory and disconnected part in public
life with detriment to his fortune, he was ready to believe
such a man to be in earnest, though not ready to believe
him to be right. In any case he lamented to see rare and
valuable qualities squandered away without any public

utility. He admitted, moreover, on the other hand, that
people frequently acquired in party confederacies a narrow,
bigoted, and proscriptive spirit. " But where duty renders
a critical situation a necessary one, it is our business to
keep free from the evils attendant upon it, and not to fly
from the situation itself. It is surely no very rational
account of a man that he has always acted right ; but
has taken special care to act in such a manner that his
endeavours could not possibly be productive of any consequence. . . . . When men are not acquainted with each
other's principles, nor experienced in each other's talents,
nor at all practised in their mutual habitudes and disposi-
tions by joint efforts of business ; no personal confidence,
no friendship, no common interest subsisting among
them ; it is evidently impossible that they can act a
public part with uniformity, perseverance, or efficacy."
    In terms of eloquent eulogy he praised the sacred reve-
rence with which the Romans used to regard the *neces-
situdo sortis*, or the relations that grew up between men who
had only held office together by the casual fortune of the
lot.   He pointed out to emulation the Whig junto who
held so close together in the reign of Anne—Sunderland,
Godolphin, Somers, and Marlborough—who believed "that
no men could act with effect who did not act in concert ;
that no men could act in concert, who did not act with
confidence ; and that no men could act with confidence,
who were not bound together by common opinions, common affections, and common interests."   In reading these
energetic passages, we have to remember two things :
first, that the writer assumes the direct object of party
combination to be generous, great, and liberal causes ;
and second, that when the time came, and when he
believed that his friends were espousing a wrong and

pernicious cause, Burke, like Samson bursting asunder
the seven green withes, broke away from the friendships
of a life, and deliberately broke his party in pieces.[1]

When Burke came to discuss the cure for the disorders
of 1770, he insisted on contenting himself with what he
ought to have known to be obviously inadequate prescriptions. And we cannot help feeling that he never speaks
of the constitution of the government of this country,
without gliding into a fallacy identical with that which he
himself described and denounced, as thinking better of the
wisdom and power of human legislation than in truth it
deserved. He was uniformly consistent in his view of the
remedies which the various sections of Opposition proposed against the existing debasement and servility of the
Lower House. The Duke of Richmond wanted universal
suffrage, equal electoral districts, and annual parliaments.
Wilkes proposed to disfranchise the rotten boroughs, to
increase the county constituencies, and to give members
to rich, populous, trading towns,—a general policy which
was accepted fifty-six years afterwards. The Constitutional Society desired frequent parliaments, the exclusion
of placemen from the House, and the increase of the county
representation. Burke uniformly refused to give his coun-
tenance to any proposals such as these, which involved a
clearly organic change in the constitution. He confessed
that he had no sort of reliance upon either a triennial
parliament or a place-bill, and with that reasonableness
which as a rule was fully as remarkable in him as his
eloquence, he showed very good grounds for his want of
faith in the popular specifics. In truth, triennial or
annual parliaments could have done no good, unless the
change had been accompanied by the more important

[1] See on the same subject, *Corresp.* ii. 276-7.

process of amputating, as Chatham called it, the rotten
boroughs. Of these the Crown could at that time reckon
some seventy as its own property. Besides those which
belonged to the Crown, there was also the immense number which belonged to the Peerage. If the king sought to
strengthen an administration, the thing needful was not
to enlist the services of able and distinguished men, but
to conciliate a duke, who brought with him the control of
a given quantity of voting power in the Lower House.
All this patrician influence, which may be found at the
bottom of most of the intrigues of the period, would not
have been touched by curtailing the duration of parliaments.

What then was the remedy, or had Burke no remedy to
offer for these grave distempers of Parliament? Only the
remedy of the interposition of the body of the people
itself. We must beware of interpreting this phrase in the
modern democratic sense. In 1766 he had deliberately
declared that he thought it would be more conformable to
the spirit of the constitution, " by lessening the number,
to add to the weight and independency of our voters."
" Considering the immense and dangerous charge of elections, the prostitute and daring venality, the corruption
of manners, the idleness and profligacy of the lower sort
of voters, no prudent man would propose to increase such
an evil." [2] In another place he denies that the people
have either enough of speculation in the closet, or of experience in business, to be competent judges, not of the detail
of particular measures only, but of *general schemes of
policy*.[3] On Burke's theory, the people, as a rule, were
no more concerned to interfere with Parliament, than a

[2] *Observations on late State of the Nation*, Works, i. 105, b.
[3] *Speech on Duration of Parliaments.*

man is concerned to interfere with somebody whom he has voluntarily and deliberately made his trustee. But here, he confessed, was a shameful and ruinous breach of trust. The ordinary rule of government was being every day mischievously contemned and daringly set aside. Until the confidence thus outraged should be once more restored, then the people ought to be excited to a more strict and detailed attention to the conduct of their representatives. The meetings of counties and cor-porations ought to settle standards for judging more systematically of the behaviour of those whom they had sent to Parliament. Frequent and correct lists of the voters in all important questions ought to be pro-cured. The severest discouragement ought to be given to the pernicious practice of affording a blind and undistinguishing support to every administration. "Par-liamentary support comes and goes with office, totally regardless of the man or the merit." For instance, Wilkes's annual motion to expunge the votes upon the Middlesex election had been uniformly rejected, as often as it was made while Lord North was in power. Lord North had no sooner given way to the Rockingham Cabinet, than the House of Commons changed its mind, and the resolutions were expunged by a handsome majo-rity of 115 to 47. Administration was omnipotent in the House, because it could be a man's most efficient friend at an election, and could most amply reward his fidelity after-wards. Against this system Burke called on the nation to set a stern face. Root it up, he kept crying ; settle the general course in which you desire members to go ; insist that they shall not suffer themselves to be diverted from this by the authority of the government of the day ; let lists of votes be published, so that you may ascertain for

yourselves whether your trustees have been faithful or
fraudulent; do all this, and there will be no need to
resort to those organic changes, those empirical innovations,
which may possibly cure, but are much more likely to
destroy.

It is not surprising that so halting a policy should have
given deep displeasure to very many, perhaps to most, of
those whose only common bond was the loose and negative
sentiment of antipathy to the court, the ministry, and
the too servile majority of the House of Commons. The
Constitutional Society was furious. Lord Chatham wrote
to Lord Rockingham that the work in which these
doctrines first appeared, must do much mischief to the
common cause. But Burke's view of the constitution was
a part of his belief with which he never paltered, and on
which he surrendered his judgment to no man. "Our
constitution," in his opinion, "stands on a nice equipoise,
with steep precipices and deep waters upon all sides of it.
In removing it from a dangerous leaning towards one side,
there may be a risk of oversetting it on the other." [4] This
image was ever before his mind. It occurs again in the
last sentence of that great protest against all change and
movement, when he describes himself as one who, when
the equipoise of the vessel in which he sails may be
endangered by overloading it upon one side, is desirous of
carrying the small weight of his reasons to that which
may preserve its equipoise. [5] When we think of the
odious misgovernment in England which the constitution
permitted, between the time when Burke wrote and the
passing of Lord Sidmouth's Six Acts fifty years later, we
may be inclined to class such a constitution among the

[4] *Present Discontents.*
[5] *Reflections on the French Revolution.*

most inadequate and mischievous political arrangements
that any free country has ever had to endure. Yet it was
this which Burke declared that he looked upon with filial
reverence. " Never will I cut it in pieces, and put it into
the kettle of any magician, in order to boil it with the
puddle of their compounds into youth and vigour; on the
contrary, I will drive away such pretenders; I will nurse
its venerable age, and with lenient arts extend a parent's
breath."

He was filled with the spirit, and he borrowed the
arguments, which have always marked the champion of
faith and authority against the impious assault of reason
or innovation. The constitution was sacred to him as the
voice of the Church and the oracles of her saints are
sacred to the faithful. Study it, he cried, until you know
how to admire it, and if you cannot know and admire,
rather believe that you are dull, than that the rest of the
world has been imposed upon. We ought to understand
it according to our measure, and to venerate where we are
not able presently to comprehend. Well has Burke been
called the Bossuet of politics.

Although, however, Burke's unflinching reverence for
the constitution, and his reluctance to lay a finger upon
it, may now seem clearly excessive, as it did to Chatham
and his son, who were great men in the right, or to
Beckford and Sawbridge, who were very little men in the
right, we can only be just to him by comparing his ideas
with those which were dominant throughout an evil
reign. While he opposed more frequent parliaments, he
still upheld the doctrine that " to govern according to the
sense, and agreeably to the interests, of the people is a
great and glorious object of government." While he
declared himself against the addition of a hundred knights

of the shire, he in the very same breath protested that,
though the people might be deceived in their choice of an
object, he " could scarcely conceive any choice they could
make, to be so very mischievous as the existence of any
human force capable of resisting it." [6] To us this may
seem very mild and commonplace doctrine, but it was not
commonplace in an age when Anglican divines—men like
Archbishop Markham, Dr. Nowell or Dr. Porteous—had
revived the base precepts of passive obedience and non-
resistance, and when such a man as Lord Mansfield
encouraged them.   And these were the kind of foundations which Burke had been laying, while Fox was yet a
Tory, while Sheridan was writing farces, and while Grey
was a schoolboy.

It is, however, almost demonstrably certain that the
vindication of the supremacy of popular interests over all
other considerations would have been bootless toil, and
that the great constitutional struggle from 1760 to 1783
would have ended otherwise than it did, but for the
failure of the war against the insurgent colonies, and the
final establishment of American Independence.   It was
this portentous transaction which finally routed the
arbitrary and despotic pretensions of the House of Commons over the people, and which put an end to the hopes
entertained by the sovereign of making his personal will
supreme in the Chambers.   Fox might well talk of an
early Loyalist victory in the war, as the terrible news
from Long Island.   The struggle which began unsuccess-
fully at Brentford in Middlesex, was continued at
Boston in Massachusetts.   The scene had changed, but
the conflicting principles were the same.   The war of
Independence was virtually a second English civil war.

    [6] *To the Chairman of the Buckinghamshire Meeting*, 1780.

The ruin of the American cause would have been also the ruin of the constitutional cause in England; and a patriotic Englishman may revere the memory of Patrick Henry and George Washington not less justly than the patriotic American. Burke's attitude in this great contest is that part of his history about the majestic and noble wisdom of which there can be least dispute.

CHAPTER IV.

THE war with the American colonies was preceded by an
interval of stupor. The violent ferment which had been
stirred in the nation by the affairs of Wilkes and the
Middlesex election, was followed, as Burke said, by as remarkable a deadness and vapidity. In 1770 the distracted
ministry of the Duke of Grafton came to an end, and was
succeeded by that of Lord North. The King had at last
triumphed. He had secured an administration of which
the fundamental principle was that the sovereign was to
be the virtual head of it, and the real director of its counsels. Lord North's government lasted for twelve years,
and its career is for ever associated with one of the most
momentous chapters in the history of the English nation
and of free institutions.

Through this long and eventful period, Burke's was as
the voice of one crying in the wilderness. He had become
important enough for the ministry to think it worth while
to take pains to discredit him. They busily encouraged
the report that he was Junius, or a close ally of Junius.
This was one of the minor vexations of Burke's middle
life. Even his friends continued to torment him for incessant disclaimers. Burke's lofty pride made him slow

to deal positively with what he scorned as a malicious and
unworthy imputation. To such a friend as Johnson he
did not, as we have seen, disdain to volunteer a denial,
but Charles Townshend was forced to write more than one
importunate letter before he could extract from Burke the
definite sentence   (Nov. 24, 1771) : — "I now give
you my word and honour that I am not the author of
Junius, and that I know not the author of that paper,
and I do authorize you to say so." Nor was this the
only kind of annoyance to which he was subjected.
His rising fame kindled the candour of the friends of
his youth. With proverbial good nature, they admo-
nished him that he did not bear instruction ; that he
showed such arrogance as in a man of his condition was
intolerable ; that he snapped furiously at his parliamentary foes, like a wolf who had broken into the fold ; that
his speeches were useless declamations ; and that he disgraced the House by the scurrilities of the bear-garden.
These sharp chastenings of friendship Burke endured with
the perfect self-command, not of the cold and indifferent
egotist, but of one who had trained himself not to expect
too much from men. He possessed the true solace for
all private chagrins in the activity and the fervour of
his public interests.

In 1772 the affairs of the East India Company, and its
relations with the Government, had fallen into disorder.
The Opposition, though powerless in the Houses of Parliament, were often able to thwart the views of the ministry in the imperial board-room in Leadenhall Street. The
Duke of Richmond was as zealous and as active in his opposition to Lord North in the business of the East Indies,
as he was in the business of the country at Westminster.
A proposal was made to Burke to go out to India at the

head of a commission of three supervisors, with authority
to examine the concerns of every department, and full
powers of control over the company's servants. Though
this offer was pressed by the directors, Burke after anxious
consideration, declined it. What his reasons were, there is
no evidence; we can only guess that he thought less of
his personal interests, than of those of the country and of
his party. Without him the Rockingham connexion would
undoubtedly have fallen to ruin, and with it the most upright, consistent, and disinterested body of men then in
public life. "You say," the Duke of Richmond wrote to
him (Nov. 15, 1772), "the party is an object of too much
importance to go to pieces. Indeed, Burke, you have
more merit than any man in keeping us together." It
was the character of the party, almost as much as their
principles, that secured Burke's zeal and attachment; their
decorum, their constancy, their aversion to all cabals for
private objects, their indifference to office, except as an in
strument of power and a means of carrying out the policy
of their convictions. They might easily have had office,
if they would have come in upon the King's terms. A
year after his fall from power, Lord Rockingham was summoned to the royal closet, and pressed to resume his post.
But office at any price was not in their thoughts. They
knew the penalties of their system, and they clung to it
undeterred. Their patriotism was deliberate and considered. Chalcedon was called the city of the blind,
because its founders wilfully neglected the more glorious
site of Byzantium which lay under their eyes. "We
have built our Chalcedon," said Burke, "with the chosen
part of the universe full in our prospect." They had the
faults to which an aristocratic party in opposition is naturally liable. Burke used to reproach them with being

somewhat languid, scrupulous, and unsystematic. He could not make the Duke of Richmond put off a large party at Goodwood for the sake of an important division in the House of Lords ; and he did not always agree with Lord John Cavendish as to what constitutes a decent and reasonable quantity of fox-hunting for a political leader in a crisis. But it was part of the steadfastness of his whole life to do his best with such materials as he could find ; he did not lose patience nor abate his effort, because his friends would miss the opportunity of a great political stroke, rather than they would miss Newmarket Races. He wrote their protests for the House of Lords, composed petitions for county meetings, drafted resolutions, and plied them with information, ideas, admonitions, and ex-hortations. Never before nor since has our country seen so extraordinary a union of the clever and indefatigable party-manager, with the reflective and philosophic habits of the speculative publicist. It is much easier to make either absolutism or democracy attractive than aristocracy ; yet we see how consistent with his deep moral conserva-tism was Burke's attachment to an aristocratic party, when we read his exhortation to the Duke of Richmond to re-member that persons in his high station in life ought to have long views. " You people," he writes to the Duke (November 17, 1772), " of great families and hereditary trusts and fortunes, are not like such as I am, who, whatever we may be, by the rapidity of our growth, and even by the fruit we bear, and flatter our-selves that, while we creep on the ground, we belly into melons that are exquisite for size and flavour, yet still we are but annual plants that perish with our season, and leave no sort of traces behind us. You, if you are what you ought to be, are in my eye the great oaks that

F

shade a country, and perpetuate your benefits from generation to generation. The immediate power of a Duke
of Richmond, or a Marquis of Rockingham, is not so much
of moment; but if their conduct and example hand down
their principles to their successors, then their houses become the public repositories and office of record for the
constitution. . . . . I do not look upon your time or lives
as lost, if in this sliding away from the genuine spirit of
the country, certain parties, if possible—if not, the heads
of certain families—should make it their business by the
whole course of their lives, principally by their example,
to mould into the very vital stamina of their descendants,
those principles which ought to be transmitted pure and
unmixed to posterity."

Perhaps such a passage as this ought to be described less
as reflection than as imagination—moral, historic, conservative imagination—in which order, social continuity,
and the endless projection of past into present, and of present into future, are clothed with the sanctity of an inner
shrine. We may think that a fox-hunting duke and a
racing marquis were very poor centres round which to
group these high emotions. But Burke had no puny sentimentalism, and none of the mere literary or romantic
conservatism of men like Chateaubriand. He lived in the
real world, and not in a false dream of some past world
that had never been. He saw that the sporting squires
of his party were as much the representatives of ancestral
force and quality, as in older days were long lines of
Claudii and Valerii. His conservative doctrine was a
profound instinct, in part political, but in greater part
moral. The accidental roughness of the symbol did not
touch him, for the symbol was glorified by the sincerity
of his faith and the compass of his imagination.

With these ideas strong within him, in 1773 Burke made a journey to France. It was almost as though the solemn hierophant of some mystic Egyptian temple should have found himself amid the brilliant chatter of a band of reckless, keen-tongued disputants of the garden or the porch at Athens. His only son had just finished a successful school-course at Westminster, and was now entered a student at Christ Church. He was still too young for the university, and Burke thought that a year could not be more profitably spent than in forming his tongue to foreign languages. The boy was placed at Auxerre, in the house of the business agent of the Bishop of Auxerre. From the Bishop he received many kindnesses, to be amply repaid in after years when the Bishop came in his old age, an exile and a beggar, to England.

While in Paris, Burke did all that he could to instruct himself as to what was going on in French society. If he had not the dazzling reception which had greeted Hume in 1764, at least he had ample opportunities of acquaint-ing himself with the prevailing ideas of the time, in more than one of the social camps into which Paris was then divided. Madame du Deffand tells the Duchess of Choi-seul that though he speaks French extremely ill, everybody felt that he would be infinitely agreeable if he could more easily make himself understood. He followed French well enough as a listener, and went every day to the courts to hear the barristers and watch the procedure. Madame du Deffand showed him all possible attention, and her friends eagerly seconded her. She invited him to supper parties where he met the Count de Broglie, the agent of the king's secret diplomacy; Caraccioli, successor of the nimble-witted Galiani as minister from Naples; and other notabilities of the high world. He supped with the

Duchess of Luxembourg, and heard a reading of La
Harpe's *Barmecides*. It was high treason in this circle to
frequent the rival salon of Mademoiselle Lespinasse, but
either the law was relaxed in the case of foreigners, or else
Burke kept his own counsel. Here were for the moment the
headquarters of the party of innovation, and here he saw
some of the men who were busily forging the thunderbolts.
His eye was on the alert, now as always, for anything
that might light up the sovereign problems of human
government. A book, by a member of this circle, had
appeared six months before, which was still the talk of
the town, and against which the government had taken
the usual impotent measures of repression. This was
the *Treatise on Tactics*, by a certain M. de Guibert, a
colonel of the Corsican legion. The important part of the
work was the introduction, in which the writer examined
with what was then thought extraordinary hardihood, the
social and political causes of the decline of the military art
in France. Burke read it with keen interest and energetic
approval. He was present at the reading of a tragedy by
the same author, and gave some offence to the rival coterie
by preferring Guibert's tragedy to La Harpe's. To us, however, of a later day, Guibert is known neither for his
tragedy nor his essay on tactics, nor for a memory so
rapid that he could open a book, throw one glance like a
flash of lightning on to a page, and then instantly repeat
from it half a dozen lines word for word. He lives in
literature as the inspirer of that ardent passion of Mademoiselle Lespinasse's letters, so unique in their consuming
intensity that, as has been said, they seem to burn the
page on which they are written. It was perhaps at
Mdlle. Lespinasse's that Burke met Diderot. The eleven
volumes of the illustrative plates of the Encyclopædia had

been given to the public twelve months before, and its
editor was just released from the giant's toil of twenty
years. Voltaire was in imperial exile at Ferney. Rousseau was copying music in a garret in the street which
is now called after his name, but he had long ago cut
himself off from society ; and Burke was not likely to take
much trouble to find out a man whom he had known in
England seven years before, and against whom he had conceived a strong and lasting antipathy, as entertaining no
principle either to influence his heart or to guide his understanding save a deranged and eccentric vanity.

It was the fashion for English visitors to go to Versailles.
They saw the dauphin and his brothers dine in public,
before a crowd of princes of the blood, nobles, abbés, and
all the miscellaneous throng of a court. They attended
mass in the chapel, where the old King, surrounded by
bishops, sat in a pew just above that of Madame du Barri.
The royal mistress astonished foreigners by hair without
powder and cheeks without rouge, the simplest toilettes,
and the most unassuming manners. Vice itself, in Burke's
famous words, seemed to lose half its evil by losing all
its grossness. And there, too, Burke had that vision to
which we owe one of the most gorgeous pages in our
literature—Marie Antoinette, the young dauphiness,
" decorating and cheering the elevated sphere she just
began to move in, glittering like the morning star, full of
life and splendour and joy." The shadow was rapidly
stealing on. The year after Burke's visit, the scene underwent a strange transformation. The King died; the mistress was banished in luxurious exile ; and the dauphiness
became the ill-starred Queen of France. Burke never
forgot the emotions of the scene; they awoke in his imagination sixteen years after, when all was changed, and

the awful contrast shook him with a passion that his
eloquence has made immortal.

Madame du Deffand wrote to Horace Walpole that
Burke had been so well received, that he ought to leave
France excellently pleased with the country. But it was
not so. His spirit was perturbed by what he had listened
to. He came away with small esteem for that busy fer-
mentation of intellect in which his French friends most
exulted, and for which they looked forward to the gratitude and admiration of posterity. From the spot on which
he stood there issued two mighty streams. It was from
the ideas of the Parisian Freethinkers whom Burke so
detested, that Jefferson, Franklin, and Henry drew those
theories of human society which were so soon to find life
in American Independence. It was from the same ideas
that later on that revolutionary tide surged forth, in which
Burke saw no elements of a blessed fertility, but only a
horrid torrent of red and desolating lava. In 1773 there
was a moment of strange repose in Western Europe, the
little break of stillness that precedes the hurricane. It
was indeed the eve of a momentous epoch. Before sixteen years were over, the American Republic had risen
like a new constellation into the firmament, and the French
monarchy, of such antiquity and fame and high pre-emi-
nence in European history, had been shattered to the dust.
We may not agree with Burke's appreciation of the forces
that were behind these vast convulsions. But at least
he saw, and saw with eyes of passionate alarm, that
strong speculative forces were at work, which must violently
prove the very bases of the great social superstructure, and
might not improbably break them up for ever.

Almost immediately after his return from France, he
sounded a shrill note of warning. Some Methodists from

Chatham had petitioned Parliament against a bill for the
relief of Dissenters from subscription to the Articles.
Burke denounced the intolerance of the petitioners. It
is not the Dissenters, he cried, whom you have to fear, but
the men who, "not contented with endeavouring to turn
your eyes from the blaze and effulgence of light, by which
life and immortality is so gloriously demonstrated by the
Gospel, would even extinguish that faint glimmering of
Nature, that only comfort supplied to ignorant man before
this great illumination. . . . . These are the people against
whom you ought to aim the shaft of the law ; these are
the men to whom, arrayed in all the terrors of government, I
would say, 'You shall not degrade us into brutes.' . . . .
The most horrid and cruel blow that can be offered to
civil society is through atheism. . . . . The infidels are
outlaws of the constitution, not of this country, but of the
human race.   They are never, never to be supported,
never to be tolerated.   Under the systematic attacks of
these people, I see some of the props of good government
already begin to fail ; I see propagated principles which
will not leave to religion even a toleration.   I see myself
sinking every day under the attacks of these wretched
people." [1]   To this pitch he had been excited by the vehement band of men, who had inscribed on their standard,
Ecraser l'Infame.

The second Parliament in which Burke had a seat, was
dissolved suddenly and without warning (October, 1774).
The attitude of America was threatening, and it was believed the Ministers were anxious to have the elections
over before the state of things became worse.   The whole
kingdom was instantly in a ferment.   Couriers, chaises,

[1] *Speech on Relief of Protestant Dissenters,* 1773.

post-horses hurried in every direction over the island, and
it was noted, as a measure of the agitation, that no fewer
than sixty messengers passed through a single turnpike on
one day. Sensible observers were glad to think that, in
consequence of the rapidity of the elections, less wine and
money would be wasted than at any election for sixty
years past. Burke had a houseful of company at Beaconsfield when the news arrived. Johnson was among them,
and as the party was hastily breaking up, the old Tory took
his Whig friend kindly by the hand ; " Farewell, my dear
sir," he said, " and remember that I wish you all the success that ought to be wished to you, and can possibly be
wished to you, by an honest man."

The words were of good omen. Burke was now rewarded
by the discovery that his labours had earned for him recognition and gratitude beyond the narrow limits of a
rather exclusive party. He had before this attracted the
attention of the mercantile public. The Company of Merchants trading to Africa voted him their thanks for his
share in supporting their establishments. The Committee
of Trade at Manchester formally returned him their grate-
ful acknowledgments for the active part that he had taken
in the business of the Jamaica free ports. But then Manchester returned no representative to Parliament. In two
Parliaments Burke had been elected for Wendover free of
expense. Lord Verney's circumstances were now so embarrassed, that he was obliged to part with the four seats
at his disposal to men who could pay for them. There
had been some talk of proposing Burke for Westminster,
and Wilkes, who was then omnipotent, promised him the
support of the popular party. But the patriot's memory
was treacherous, and he speedily forgot, for reasons of his
own, an idea that had originated with himself. Burke's

constancy of spirit was momentarily overclouded. "Sometimes when I am alone," he wrote to Lord Rockingham
(September 15, 1774), "in spite of all my efforts, I fall
into a melancholy which is inexpressible, and to which, if
I gave way, I should not continue long under it, but must
totally sink. Yet I do assure you that partly, and indeed
principally, by the force of natural good spirits, and partly
by a strong sense of what I ought to do, I bear up so well
that no one who did not know them, could easily discover
the state of my mind or my circumstances. I have those
that are dear to me, for whom I must live as long as God
pleases, and in what way he pleases. Whether I ought
not totally to abandon this public station for which I am so
unfit, and have of course been so unfortunate, I know not."
But he was always saved from rash retirement from public
business by two reflections. He doubted whether a man
has a right to retire after he has once gone a certain
length in these things. And he remembered that there
are often obscure vexations in the most private life, which
as effectually destroy a man's peace as anything that can
occur in public contentions.

Lord Rockingham offered his influence on behalf of
Burke at Malton, one of the family boroughs in
Yorkshire, and thither Burke in no high spirits betook
himself. On his way to the north he heard that he had
been nominated for Bristol, but the nomination had, for
certain electioneering reasons, not been approved by the
party. As it happened, Burke was no sooner chosen
at Malton than, owing to an unexpected turn of affairs at
Bristol, the idea of proposing him for a candidate revived.
Messengers were sent express to his house in London,
and, not finding him there, they hastened down to Yorkshire. Burke quickly resolved that the offer was too im-

portant to be rejected. Bristol was the capital of the west,
and it was still in wealth, population, and mercantile activity the second city of the kingdom. To be invited to
stand for so great a constituency, without any request of his
own and free of personal expense, was a distinction which
no politician could hold lightly. Burke rose from the
table where he was dining with some of his supporters,
stepped into a post-chaise at six on a Tuesday evening,
and travelled without a break until he reached Bristol on
the Thursday afternoon, having got over two hundred and
seventy miles in forty-four hours. Not only did he execute the journey without a break, but, as he told the people
of Bristol, with an exulting commemoration of his own
zeal that recalls Cicero, he did not sleep for an instant in the
interval. The poll was kept open for a month, and the
contest was the most tedious that had ever been known in
the city. New freemen were admitted down to the very
last day of the election. At the end of it, Burke was
second on the poll, and was declared to be duly chosen
(November 3, 1774). There was a petition against his
return, but the election was confirmed, and he continued
to sit for Bristol for six years.

The situation of a candidate is apt to find out a man's
weaker places. Burke stood the test. He showed none
of the petulant rage of those clamorous politicians whose
flight, as he säid, is winged in a lower region of the air.
As the traveller stands on the noble bridge that now spans
the valley of the Avon, he may recall Burke's local comparison of these busy, angry familiars of an election, to
the gulls that skim the mud of the river when it is ex-
hausted of its tide. He gave his new friends a more important lesson, when the time came for him to thank them
for the honour which they had just conferred upon him.

His colleague had opened the subject of the relations between a member of Parliament and his constituents ; and
had declared that, for his own part, he should regard the
instructions of the people of Bristol as decisive and binding.
Burke in a weighty passage upheld a manlier doctrine.

" Certainly, gentlemen, it ought to be the happiness and glory
of a representative to live in the strictest union, the closest correspondence, and the most unreserved communication with his
constituents.   Their wishes ought to have great weight with him ;
their opinions high respect, their business unremitted attention.
It is his duty to sacrifice his repose, his pleasure, his satisfactions,
to theirs ; and above all, ever, and in all cases, to prefer their interest to his own. But his unbiassed opinion, his mature judgment,
his enlightened conscience, he ought not to sacrifice to you, to any
man, or to any set of men living.   Your representative owes you,
not his industry only, but his judgment ; and he betrays, instead
of serving you, if he sacrifices it to your opinion.
" My worthy colleague says, his will ought to be subservient
to yours.   If that be all, the thing is innocent.   If government
were a matter of will upon any side, yours, without question,
ought to be superior.   But government and legislation are matters of reason and judgment, and not of inclination ; and what
sort of reason is that in which the determination precedes
the discussion, in which one set of men deliberate and another
decide, and where those who form the conclusion are perhaps
three hundred miles distant from those who hear the arguments ? . . . . *Authoritative* instructions, *mandates* issued,
which the member is bound blindly and implicitly to obey, to
vote, and to argue for, though contrary to the clearest convictions
of his judgment and conscience—these are things utterly unknown
to the laws of this land, and which arise from a fundamental mistake of the whole order and tenour of our Constitution." [2]

For six years the Bristol electors were content to be
represented by a man of this independence.   They never,
however, really acquiesced in the principle that a member
of Parliament owes as much to his own convictions as to

[2] *Speech at the conclusion of the Poll.*

the will of his constituents. In 1778 a bill was brought
into Parliament, relaxing some of the restrictions imposed
upon Ireland by the atrocious fiscal policy of Great Britain. The great mercantile centres raised a furious outcry,
and Bristol was as blind and as boisterous as Manchester
and Glasgow. Burke not only spoke and voted in favour
of the commercial propositions, but urged that the proposed removal of restrictions on Irish trade did not go
nearly far enough. There was none of that too familiar
casuistry, by which public men argue themselves out of
their consciences in a strange syllogism, that they can
best serve the country in Parliament; that to keep their
seats they must follow their electors; and that therefore,
in the long run, they serve the country best by acqui-
escing in ignorance and prejudice. Anybody can denounce an abuse. It needs valour and integrity to stand
forth against a wrong to which our best friends are most
ardently committed. It warms our hearts to think of the
noble courage with which Burke faced the blind and vile
selfishness of his own supporters. He reminded them that
England only consented to leave to the Irish, in two or three
instances, the use of the natural faculties which God had
given them. He asked them whether Ireland was united
to Great Britain for no other purpose than that we should
counteract the bounty of Providence in her favour; and
whether, in proportion as that bounty had been liberal, we
were to regard it as an evil to be met with every possible
corrective? In our day there is nobody of any school who
doubts that Burke's view of our trade policy towards Ireland was accurately, absolutely, and magnificently right.
I need not repeat the arguments. They made no mark
on the Bristol merchants. Burke boldly told them that
he would rather run the risk of displeasing than of injuring

them.   They implored him to become their advocate.
" I should only disgrace myself," he said ; " I should lose
the only thing which can make such abilities as mine of
any use to the world now or hereafter.   I mean that
authority which is derived from the opinion that a member speaks the language of truth and sincerity, and that
he is not ready to take up or lay down a great political
system for the convenience of the hour ; that he is in
Parliament to support his opinion of the public good, and
does not form his opinion in order to get into Parliament
or to continue in it."[3]

A small instalment of humanity to Ireland was not
more distasteful to the electors of Bristol, than a small
instalment of toleration to Roman Catholics in England.   A measure was passed (1778) repealing certain iniquitous penalties created by an Act of William
the Third.   It is needless to say that this rudimentary
concession to justice and sense was supported by Burke.
His voters began to believe that those were right who had
said that he had been bred at Saint Omer's, was a Papist
at heart, and a Jesuit in disguise.   When the time came,
summa dies et ineluctabile fatum, Burke bore with dignity
and temper his dismissal from the only independent constituency that he ever represented.   Years before he had
warned a young man entering public life, to regard and
wish well to the common people, whom his best instincts
and his highest duties lead him to love and to serve, but
to put as little trust in them as in princes.   Burke some-
where describes an honest public life as carrying on a poor
unequal conflict against the passions and prejudices of our
day, perhaps with no better weapons than passions and
prejudices of our own.

[3] *Two Letters to Gentlemen in Bristol,* 1778.

The six years during which Burke sat in Parliament
for Bristol, saw this conflict carried on under the most
desperate circumstances. They were the years of the
civil war between the English at home and the English
in the American colonies. George III. and Lord North
have been made scapegoats for sins which were not exclusively their own. They were only the organs and
representatives of all the lurking ignorance and arbitrary
humours of the entire community. Burke discloses in
many places, that for once the King and Parliament did
not act without the sympathies of the mass. In his
famous speech at Bristol, in 1780, he was rebuking the
intolerance of those who bitterly taunted him for the
support of the measure for the relaxation of the Penal
Code. "It is but too true," he said in a passage worth
remembering, "that the love, and even the very idea,
of genuine liberty is extremely rare. It is but too true
that there are many whose whole scheme of freedom is
made up of pride, perverseness, and insolence. They
feel themselves in a state of thraldom, they imagine that
their souls are cooped and cabined in, unless they have
some man, or some body of men, dependent on their
mercy. The desire of having some one below them,
descends to those who are the very lowest of all ; and a
Protestant cobbler, debased by his poverty, but exalted
by his share of the ruling church, feels a pride in knowing it is by his generosity alone that the peer, whose
footman's instep he measures, is able to keep his chaplain
from a gaol. This disposition is the true source of the
passion which many men, in very humble life, have taken
to the American war. *Our* subjects in America ; *our*
colonies ; *our* dependents. This lust of party power is
the liberty they hunger and thirst for ; and this Siren

song of ambition has charmed ears that we would have
thought were never organized to that sort of music."

This was the mental attitude of a majority of the nation,
and it was fortunate for them and for us that the yeomen and
merchants on the other side of the Atlantic had a more
just and energetic appreciation of the crisis. The insurgents, while achieving their own freedom, were indirectly
engaged in fighting the battle of the people of the mother
country as well. Burke had a vehement correspondent
who wrote to him (1777), that if the utter ruin of this
country were to be the consequence of her persisting in
the claim to tax America, then he would be the first to
say, *Let her perish!* If England prevails, said Horace
Walpole, English and American liberty is at an end ; if
one fell, the other would fall with it. Burke, seeing this,
" certainly never could and never did wish," as he says of
himself, "the colonists to be subdued by arms. He was
fully persuaded that if such should be the event, they
must be held in that subdued state by a great body of
standing forces, and perhaps of foreign forces. He was
strongly of opinion that such armies, first victorious over
Englishmen, in a conflict for English constitutional rights
and privileges, and afterwards habituated (though in
America) to keep an English people in a state of abject
subjection, would prove fatal in the end to the liberties
of England itself."[4] The way for this remote peril was
being sedulously prepared by a widespread deterioration
among popular ideas, and a fatal relaxation of the hold
which they had previously gained in the public mind.
In order to prove that the Americans had no right to
their liberties, we were every day endeavouring to subvert
the maxims which preserve the whole spirit of our own.

[4] *Appeal from the new to the old Whigs.*

To prove that the Americans ought not to be free, we were
obliged to depreciate the value of freedom itself. The
material strength of the Government, and its moral strength
alike, would have been reinforced by the defeat of the
colonists, to such an extent as to have seriously delayed
or even jeopardized English progress, and therefore that
of Europe too. As events actually fell out, the ferocious
administration of the law in the last five or six years of
the eighteenth century, was the retribution for the lethargy
or approval with which the mass of the English community
had watched the measures of the government against their
fellow-Englishmen in America.

It is not necessary here to follow Burke minutely
through the successive stages of parliamentary action in
the American war. He always defended the settlement
of 1766 ; the Stamp Act was repealed, and the constitutional supremacy and sovereign authority of the mother-
country was preserved in a Declaratory Act. When the
project of taxing the colonies was revived, and relations
with them were becoming strained and dangerous, Burke
came forward with a plan for leaving the General Assem-
blies of the colonies to grant supplies and aids, instead
of giving and granting supplies in Parliament, to be raised
and paid in the colonies. Needless to say that it was rejected, and perhaps it was not feasible. Henceforth
Burke could only watch in impotence the blunders of
government, and the disasters that befell the national arms.
But his protests against the war will last as long as our
literature.

Of all Burke's writings none are so fit to secure unqualified and unanimous admiration as the three pieces on this
momentous struggle :—the Speech on American Taxation
(April 19, 1774) ; the Speech on Conciliation with

America (March 22, 1775); and the Letter to the Sheriffs
of Bristol (1777).   Together they hardly exceed the compass of the little volume which the reader now has in his
hands.   It is no exaggeration to say that they compose
the most perfect manual in our literature, or in any
literature, for one who approaches the study of public
affairs, whether for knowledge or for practice.   They are
an example without fault of all the qualities which the
critic, whether a theorist or an actor, of great political
situations should strive by night and by day to possess.
If the subject with which they deal were less near than it
is to our interests and affections as free citizens, these three
performances would still abound in the lessons of an incomparable political method.   If their subject were as remote
as the quarrel between the Corinthians and Corcyra, or
the war between Rome and the Allies, instead of a conflict
to which the world owes the opportunity of the most
important of political experiments, we should still have
everything to learn from the author's treatment; the
vigorous grasp of masses of compressed detail, the wide
illumination from great principles of human experience,
the strong and masculine feeling for the two great political
ends of Justice and Freedom, the large and generous
interpretation of expediency, the morality, the vision, the
noble temper.   If ever, in the fulness of time, and surely
the fates of men and literature cannot have it otherwise,
Burke becomes one of the half-dozen names of established
and universal currency in education and in common books,
rising above the waywardness of literary caprice or intellectual fashions, as Shakespeare and Milton and Bacon
rise above it, it will be the mastery, the elevation,
the wisdom, of these far-shining discourses in which the

world will in an especial degree recognize the combination of sovereign gifts with beneficent uses.

The pamphlet on the *Present Discontents* is partially
obscured or muffled to the modern reader, by the space
which is given to the cabal of the day. The *Reflections
on the French Revolution* over-abounds in declamation,
and—apart from its being passionately on one side, and
that perhaps the wrong one—the splendour of the eloquence
is out of proportion to the reason and the judgment. In the
pieces on the American war, on the contrary, Burke was
conscious that he could trust nothing to the sympathy or
the prepossessions of his readers, and this put him upon an
unwonted persuasiveness. Here it is reason and judgment,
not declamation ; lucidity, not passion ; that produces
the effects of eloquence. No choler mars the page ; no
purple patch distracts our minds from the penetrating
force of the argument ; no commonplace is dressed up into
a vague sublimity. The cause of freedom is made to wear
its own proper robe of equity, self-control, and reasonableness.

Not one, but all those great idols of the political market-
place whose worship and service has cost the race so dear,
are discovered and shown to be the foolish uncouth stocks
and stones that they are. Fox once urged members of parliament to peruse the speech on Conciliation again and again,
to study it, to imprint it on their minds, to impress it on
their hearts. But Fox only referred to the lesson which
he thought to be contained in it, that representation is the
sovereign remedy for every evil. This is by far the least
important of its lessons. It is great in many ways. It is
greatest as a remonstrance and an answer against the thriv-
ing sophisms of barbarous national pride, the eternal fallacies
of war and conquest ; and here it is great, as all the three

pieces on the subject are so, because they expose with unanswerable force the deep-lying faults of heart and temper,
as well as of understanding, which move nations to haughty
and violent courses.

The great argument with those of the war party who
pretended to a political defence of their position, was the
doctrine that the English government was sovereign in
the colonies as at home ; and in the notion of sovereignty
they found inherent the notion of an indefeasible right
to impose and exact taxes. Having satisfied themselves
of the existence of this sovereignty, and of the right
which they took to be its natural property, they saw no
step between the existence of an abstract right, and the
propriety of enforcing it.   We have seen an instance of
a similar mode of political thinking in our own lifetime.
During the great civil war between the northern and
southern states of the American Union, people in England
convinced themselves—some after careful examination of
documents, others by cursory glances at second-hand
authorities—that the south had a right to secede. The
current of opinion was precisely similar in the struggle
to which the United States owed their separate existence.
Now the idea of a right as a mysterious and reverend
abstraction, to be worshipped in a state of naked divorce
from expediency and convenience, was one that Burke's
political judgment found preposterous and unendurable.
He hated the arbitrary and despotic savour which clung
about the English assumptions over the colonies. And
his repulsion was heightened when he found that these
assumptions were justified, not by some permanent advantage which their victory would procure for the mother
country or for the colonies, or which would repay the
cost of gaining such a victory; not by the assertion and

demonstration of some positive duty, but by the futile
and meaningless doctrine that we had a right to do something or other, if we liked.

The alleged compromise of the national dignity implied
in a withdrawal of the just claim of the government,
instead of convincing, only exasperated him. " Show the
thing you contend for to be reason ; show it to be common
sense ; show it to be the means of attaining some useful
end ; and then I am content to allow it what dignity you
please."⁵ The next year he took up the ground still more
firmly, and explained it still more impressively. As for
the question of the right of taxation, he exclaimed, " It
is less than nothing in my consideration. . . . . My consideration is narrow, confined, and wholly limited to the
policy of the question. I do not examine whether the
giving away a man's money be a power excepted and
reserved out of the general trust of Government. . . . .
*The question with me is not whether you have a right to
render your people miserable, but whether it is not your
interest to make them happy.* It is not what a lawyer
tells me I *may* do, but what humanity, reason, and justice
tell me I *ought* to do. I am not determining a point of
law ; I am restoring tranquillity, and the general character
and situation of a people must determine what sort of
government is fitted for them." " I am not here going
into the distinctions of rights," he cries, " not attempting
to mark their boundaries. I do not enter into these
metaphysical distinctions. *I hate the very sound of them.*
This is the true touchstone of all theories which regard
man and the affairs of man : does it suit his nature in
general ?—does it suit his nature as modified by his
habits ?" He could not bear to think of having legis-

⁵ *Speech on American Taxation.*

lative or political arrangements shaped or vindicated by a delusive geometrical accuracy of deduction, instead of being entrusted to "the natural operation of things, which, left to themselves, generally fall into their proper order."

Apart from his incessant assertion of the principle that man acts from adequate motives relative to his interests, and not on metaphysical speculations, Burke sows, as he marches along in his stately argument, many a germ of the modern philosophy of civilization. He was told that America was worth fighting for. "Certainly it is," he answered, "if fighting a people be the best way of gaining them." Every step that has been taken in the direction of progress, not merely in empire, but in education, in punishment, in the treatment of the insane, has shown the deep wisdom, so unfamiliar in that age of ferocious penalties and brutal methods, of this truth,—that "the natural effect of fidelity, clemency, kindness in governors, is peace, good-will, order, and esteem in the governed." Is there a single instance to the contrary? Then there is that sure key to wise politics :—"*Nobody shall persuade me when a whole people are concerned, that acts of lenity are not means of conciliation.*" And that still more famous sentence, "*I do not know the method of drawing up an indictment against a whole people.*"

Good and observant men will feel that no misty benevolence or vague sympathy, but the positive reality of experience, inspired such passages as that where he says,—"Never expecting to find perfection in men, and not looking for divine attributes in created beings, in my commerce with my contemporaries I have found much human virtue. The age unquestionably produces daring profligates and insidious hypocrites? What then? Am I not to avail myself of whatever good is to be found in

the world, because of the mixture of evil that is in it!
. . . . Those who raise suspicions of the good, on account
of the behaviour of evil men, are of the party of the
latter. . . . A conscientious person would rather doubt
his own judgment, than condemn his species. He that
accuses all mankind of corruption, ought to remember
that he is sure to convict only one. In truth I should
much rather admit those whom at any time I have dis-
relished the most, to be patterns of perfection, than seek
a consolation to my own unworthiness in a general com-
munion of depravity with all about me." This is one
of those pieces of rational constancy and mental wholeness
in Burke, which fill up our admiration for him—one of
the manifold illustrations of an invincible fidelity to the
natural order and operation of things, even when they
seemed most hostile to all that was dear to his own
personality.

CHAPTER V

TOWARDS 1780 it began to be clear that the ministers had
brought the country into disaster and humiliation, from
which their policy contained no way of escape. In the
closing months of the American war, the Opposition
pressed ministers with a vigour that never abated. Lord
North bore their attacks with perfect good humour.
When Burke, in the course of a great oration, parodied
Burgoyne's invitation to the Indians to repair to the
King's standard, the wit and satire of it almost suffo-
cated the prime minister, not with shame but with
laughter. His heart had long ceased to be in the
matter, and everybody knew that he only retained his
post in obedience to the urgent importunities of the
king, whilst such colleagues as Rigby only clung to
their place because the salaries were endeared by long
familiarity. The general gloom was accidentally deepened
by that hideous outbreak of fanaticism and violence,
which is known as the Lord George Gordon Riots
(June, 1780). The Whigs, as having favoured the relaxation of the laws against popery, were especially obnoxious
to the mob. The government sent a guard of soldiers
to protect Burke's house in Charles Street, St. James's;

but, after he had removed the more important of his papers, he insisted on the guard being dispatched for the protection of more important places, and he took shelter under the roof of General Burgoyne. His excellent wife, according to a letter of his brother, had "the firmness and sweetness of an angel; but why do I say of an angel?—of a woman." Burke himself courageously walked to and fro amid the raging crowds with firm composure, though the experiment was full of peril. He describes the mob as being made up, as London mobs generally are, rather of the unruly and dissolute than of fanatical malignants, and he vehemently opposed any concessions by Parliament to the spirit of intolerance which had first kindled the blaze. All the letters of the time show that the outrages and alarms of those days and nights, in which the capital seemed to be at the mercy of a furious rabble, made a deeper impression on the minds of contemporaries than they ought to have done. Burke was not likely to be less excited than others, by the sight of such insensate disorder; and it is no idle fancy that he had the mobs of 1780 still in his memory, when ten years later he poured out the vials of his wrath on the bloodier mob which carried the King and Queen of France in wild triumph from Versailles to Paris.

In the previous February (1780) Burke had achieved one of the greatest of all his parliamentary and oratorical successes. Though the matter of this particular enterprise is no longer alive, yet it illustrates his many strong qualities in so remarkable a way that it is right to give some account of it. We have already seen that Burke steadily set his face against parliamentary reform; he habitually declared that the machine was well enough to answer any good purpose, provided the materials were

sound. The statesman who resists all projects for the
reform of the constitution, and yet eagerly proclaims how
deplorably imperfect are the practical results of its working,
binds himself to vigorous exertions for the amendment
of administration. Burke devoted himself to this duty
with a fervid assiduity that has not often been exampled,
and has never been surpassed. He went to work with
the zeal of a religious enthusiast, intent on purging his
church and his faith of the corruptions which lowered it
in the eyes of men. There was no part or order of
government so obscure, so remote, or so complex, as to
escape his acute and persevering observation.

Burke's object, in his schemes for Economical Reform,
was less to husband the public resources and relieve the
tax-payer—though this aim could not have been absent
from his mind, overburdened as England then was with
the charges of the American War—than to cut off the
channels which supplied the corruption of the House of
Commons. The full title of the first project which he
presented to the legislature (February, 1780), was A Plan
for the Better Security of the Independence of Parliament, and the Economical Reformation of the Civil and
other Establishments. It was to the former that he
deemed the latter to be the most direct road. The
strength of the administration in the House was due to
the gifts which the Minister had in his hands to dispense.
Men voted with the side which could reward their fidelity.
It was the number of sinecure places and unpublished
pensions, which along with the controllable influence of
peers and nabobs, furnished the Minister with an irresistible lever : the avarice and the degraded public spirit
of the recipients supplied the required fulcrum. Burke
knew that in sweeping away these factitious places and

secret pensions, he would be robbing the Court of its
chief implements of corruption, and protecting the representative against his chief motive in selling his country.
He conceived that he would thus be promoting a far more
infallible means than any scheme of electoral reform
could have provided, for reviving the integrity and independence of the House of Commons. In his eyes, the
evil resided not in the constituencies, but in their representatives; not in the small number of the one, but in
the smaller integrity of the other.

The evil did not stop where it began. It was not
merely that the sinister motive, thus engendered in the
minds of too lax and facile men, induced them to betray
their legislative trust, and barter their own uprightness
and the interests of the State. The acquisition of one of
these nefarious bribes meant much more than a sinister
vote. It called into existence a champion of every in-
veterate abuse that weighed on the resources of the
country. There is a well-known passage in the speech
on Economical Reform, in which the speaker shows what
an insurmountable obstacle Lord Talbot had found in his
attempt to carry out certain reforms in the royal household, in the fact that the turnspit of the King's kitchen
was a member of Parliament. "On that rock his whole
adventure split,—his whole scheme of economy was
dashed to pieces; his department became more expensive
than ever; the Civil List debt accumulated." Inter-
ference with the expenses of the household meant inter-
ference with the perquisites or fees of this legislative
turnspit, and the rights of sinecures were too sacred to be
touched. In comparison with them, it counted for
nothing that the King's tradesmen went unpaid, and
became bankrupt; that the judges were unpaid; that

"the justice of the kingdom bent and gave way; the
foreign ministers remained inactive and unprovided; the
system of Europe was dissolved; the chain of our alli-
ances was broken; all the wheels of Government at home
and abroad were stopped. *The king's turnspit was a
member of Parliament.*" [1] This office and numbers of
others exactly like it, existed solely because the House of
Commons was crowded with venal men. The post of
royal scullion meant a vote that could be relied upon
under every circumstance and in all emergencies. And
each incumbent of such an office felt his honour and
interests concerned in the defence of all other offices of
the same scandalous description. There was thus maintained a strong standing army of expensive, lax, and
corrupting officials.

The royal household was a gigantic nest of costly
jobbery and purposeless profusion. It retained all "the
cumbrous charge of a Gothic establishment," though all
its usage and accommodation had "shrunk into the
polished littleness of modern elegance." The outlay was
enormous. The expenditure on the court tables only was
a thing unfathomable. Waste was the rule in every
branch of it. There was an office for the Great Wardrobe,
another office of the Robes, a third of the Groom of the
Stole. For these three useless offices there were three
useless treasurers. They all laid a heavy burden on the
taxpayer, in order to supply a bribe to the member of
parliament. The plain remedy was to annihilate the

---

[1] The Civil List at this time comprehended a great number of
charges, such as those of which Burke speaks, that had nothing
to do with the sovereign personally. They were slowly removed,
the judicial and diplomatic charges being transferred on the
accession of William IV.

subordinate treasuries. "Take away," was Burke's
demand, "the whole establishment of detail in the household : the Treasurer, the Comptroller, the Cofferer of the
Household, the Treasurer of the Chamber, the Master of
the Household, the whole Board of Green Cloth ; a vast
number of subordinate offices in the department of the
Steward of the Household ; the whole establishment of
the Great Wardrobe ; the Removing Wardrobe ; the
Jewel Office ; the Robes ; the Board of Works." The
abolition of this confused and costly system would not
only diminish expense and promote efficiency ; it would
do still more excellent service in destroying the roots of
parliamentary corruption. " Under other governments
a question of expense is only a question of economy,
and it is nothing more ; with us, in every question
of expense, there is always a mixture of constitutional
considerations."

Places and pensions, though the worst, were not by
any means the only stumbling-block in the way of pure
and well-ordered government. The administration of the
estates of the Crown,—the Principality, the Duchy of
Cornwall, the Duchy of Lancaster, the County Palatine
of Chester,—was an elaborate system of obscure and
unprofitable expenditure. Wales had to herself eight
judges, while no more than twelve sufficed to perform the
whole business of justice in England, a country ten times
as large, and a hundred times as opulent. Wales, and
each of the duchies, had its own exchequer. Every one
of these principalities, said Burke, has the apparatus of a
kingdom, for the jurisdiction over a few private estates ;
it has the formality and charge of the Exchequer of Great
Britain, for collecting the rents of a country squire. They
were the field, in his expressive phrase, of mock juris-

dictions and mimic revenues, of difficult trifles and
laborious fooleries. " It was but the other day that
that pert factious fellow, the Duke of Lancaster, presumed to fly in the face of his liege lord, our gracious
sovereign—presumed to go to law with the King. The
object is neither your business nor mine. Which of the
parties got the better I really forget. The material point
is that the suit cost about 15,000l. But as the Duke of
Lancaster is but agent of Duke Humphrey, and not worth
a groat, our sovereign was obliged to pay the costs of
both." The system which involved these costly absurdities,
Burke proposed entirely to abolish. In the same spirit
he wished to dispose of the Crown lands and the forest
lands, which it was for the good of the community, not
less than of the Crown itself, to throw into the hands of
private owners.

One of the most important of these projected reforms,
and one which its author did not flinch from carrying out
two years later to his own loss, related to the office of
Paymaster. This functionary was accustomed to hold
large balances of the public money in his own hands
and for his own profit, for long periods, owing to a
complex system of accounts which was so rigorous as
entirely to defeat its own object. The Paymaster could
not, through the multiplicity of forms and the exaction
of impossible conditions, get a prompt acquittance. The
audit sometimes did not take place for years after the
accounts were virtually closed. Meanwhile, the money
accumulated in his hands, and its profits were his legitimate perquisite. The first Lord Holland, for example,
held the balances of his office from 1765, when he
retired, until 1778, when they were audited. During this
time he realized, as the interest on the use of these

balances, nearly two hundred and fifty thousand pounds.
Burke diverted these enormous gains into the coffers of
the state.   He fixed the Paymaster's salary at four
thousand pounds a year, and was himself the first person
who accepted the curtailed income.

Not the most fervid or brilliant of Burke's pieces, yet
the Speech on Economical Reform is certainly not the least
instructive or impressive of them.   It gives a suggestive
view of the relations existing at that time between the
House of Commons and the Court.   It reveals the narrow
and unpatriotic spirit of the King and the ministers,
who could resist proposals so reasonable in themselves,
and so remedial in their effects, at a time when the nation
was suffering the heavy and distressing burdens of the
most disastrous war that our country has ever carried on.
It is especially interesting as an illustration of its author's
political capacity.   At a moment when committees, and
petitions, and great county meetings showed how
thoroughly the national anger was roused against the
existing system, Burke came to the front of affairs with a
scheme, of which the most striking characteristic proved
to be that it was profoundly temperate.   Bent on the
extirpation of the system, he had no ill-will towards the
men who had happened to flourish in it.   " I never will
suffer," he said, " any man or description of men to suffer
from errors that naturally have grown out of the abusive
constitution of those offices which I propose to regulate.
If I cannot reform with equity, I will not reform at all."
Exasperated as he was by the fruitlessness of his opposition
to a policy which he detested from the bottom of his
soul, it would have been little wonderful if he had
resorted to every weapon of his unrivalled rhetorical
armoury, in order to discredit and overthrow the whole

scheme of government. Yet nothing could have been
further from his mind than any violent or extreme idea of
this sort. Many years afterwards he took credit to himself less for what he did on this occasion, than for what
he prevented from being done. People were ready for a
new modelling of the two Houses of Parliament, as well
as for grave modifications of the Prerogative. Burke
resisted this temper unflinchingly. " I had," he says,
" a state to preserve, as well as a state to reform. I had
a people to gratify, but not to inflame or to mislead."
He then recounts without exaggeration the pains and
caution with which he sought reform, while steering clear
of innovation. He heaved the lead every inch of way he
made. It is grievous to think that a man who could
assume such an attitude at such a time, who could give
this kind of proof of his skill in the great, the difficult,
art of governing, only held a fifth-rate office for some time
less than a twelvemonth.

The year of the project of Economic Reform (1780) is
usually taken as the date when Burke's influence and repute
were at their height. He had not been tried in the fire of
official responsibility, and his impetuosity was still under
a degree of control which not long afterwards was fatally
weakened by an over-mastering irritability of constitution.
High as his character was now in the ascendant, it was in
the same year that Burke suffered the sharp mortification
of losing his seat at Bristol. His speech before the election is one of the best known of all his performances ;
and it well deserves to be so, for it is surpassed by none
in gravity, elevation, and moral dignity. We can only
wonder that a constituency which could suffer itself to be
addressed on this high level, should have allowed the
small selfishness of local interest to weigh against such

wisdom and nobility. But Burke soon found in the course
of his canvas that he had no chance, and he declined to
go to the poll. On the previous day one of his competi-
tors had fallen down dead. " *What shadows we are,*"
said Burke, "*and what shadows we pursue !* "

In 1782 Lord North's government came to an end, and
the king "was pleased," as Lord North quoted with
jesting irony from the Gazette, to send for Lord Rockingham, Charles Fox, and Lord Shelburne. Members could
hardly believe their own eyes, as they saw Lord North and
the members of a government which had been in place for
twelve years, now lounging on the opposition benches in
their greatcoats, frocks, and boots, while Fox and Burke
shone in the full dress that was then worn by ministers, and
cut unwonted figures with swords, lace, and hair powder.
Sheridan was made an under-secretary of state, and to the
younger Pitt was offered his choice of various minor posts,
which he haughtily refused. Burke, to whom on their
own admission the party owed everything, was appointed
Paymaster of the Forces, with a salary of four thousand
pounds a year. His brother, Richard Burke, was made
Secretary of the Treasury. His son, Richard, was named
to be his father's deputy at the Pay Office, with a salary
of five hundred pounds a year.

This singular exclusion from cabinet office of the most
powerful genius of the party, has naturally given rise to
abundant criticism ever since. It will be convenient
to say what there is to be said on this subject, in
connexion with the events of 1788, (below, p. 138)
because there happens to exist some useful information
about the ministerial crisis of that year, which sheds a
clearer light upon the arrangements of six years before.
Meanwhile it is enough to say that Burke himself had

most reasonably looked to some higher post. There is the distinct note of the humility of mortified pride in a letter written in reply to some one who had applied to him for a place. "You have been misinformed," he says; "I make no part of the ministerial arrangement. Something in the official line may possibly be thought fit for my measure." Burke knew that his position in the country entitled him to something above the official line. In a later year, when he felt himself called upon to defend his pension, he described what his position was in the momentous crisis from 1780 to 1782, and Burke's habitual veraciousness forbids us to treat the description as in any way exaggerated. "By what accident it matters not," he says, "nor upon what desert, but just then, and in the midst of that hunt of obloquy which has ever pursued me with a full cry through life, I had obtained a very full degree of public confidence. . . . . Nothing to prevent disorder was omitted; when it appeared, nothing to subdue it was left uncounselled nor unexecuted, as far as I could prevail. At the time I speak of, and having a momentary lead, so aided and so encouraged, and as a feeble instrument in a mighty hand—I do not say I saved my country—I am sure I did my country important service. There were few indeed that did not at that time acknowledge it—and that time was thirteen years ago. It was but one view, that no man in the kingdom better deserved an honourable provision should be made for him." [2]

We have seen that Burke had fixed the Paymaster's salary at four thousand pounds, and had destroyed the extravagant perquisites. The other economical reforms which were actually effected, fell short by a long way of those

[2] *Letter to a Noble Lord.*

H

which Burke had so industriously devised and so forcibly
recommended. In 1782, while Burke declined to spare
his own office, the chief of the cabinet conferred upon
Barré a pension of over three thousand a year; above
ten times the amount, as has been said, which, in
Lord Rockingham's own judgment, as expressed in the
new Bill, ought henceforth to be granted to any one
person whatever. This shortcoming, however, does not
detract from Burke's merit. He was not responsible for
it. The eloquence, ingenuity, diligence, above all, the
sagacity and the justice of this great effort of 1780, are
none the less worthy of our admiration and regard because,
in 1782, his chiefs, partly perhaps out of a newborn
deference for the feelings of their royal master, showed
that the possession of office had sensibly cooled the ardent
aspirations proper to Opposition.

The events of the twenty months between the resignation of Lord North (1782) and the accession of Pitt to
the office of Prime Minister (December, 1783,) mark an
important crisis in political history, and they mark an
important crisis in Burke's career and hopes. Lord Rockingham had just been three months in office, when he died
(July, 1782). This dissolved the bond that held the two
sections of the ministry together, and let loose a flood of
rival ambitions and sharp animosities. Lord Shelburne
believed himself to have an irresistible claim to the
chief post in the administration; among other reasons,
because he might have had it before Lord Rockingham
three months earlier, if he had so chosen. The King supported him, not from any partiality to his person, but
because he dreaded and hated Charles Fox. The character of Shelburne is one of the perplexities of the time.
His views on peace and free trade make him one of the

precursors of the Manchester School. No minister was so
well informed as to the threads of policy in foreign countries. He was the intimate or the patron of men who
now stand out as among the first lights of that time—
of Morellet, of Priestley, of Bentham. Yet a few months
of power seem to have disclosed faults of character, which
left him without a single political friend, and blighted him
with irreparable discredit. Fox, who was now the head
of the Rockingham section of the Whigs, had, before the
death of the late premier, been on the point of refusing to
serve any longer with Lord Shelburne, and he now very
promptly refused to serve under him. When Parliament
met after Rockingham's death, gossips noticed that Fox
and Burke continued, long after the Speaker had taken the
chair, to walk backwards and forwards in the Court of
Requests, engaged in earnest conversation. According to
one story, Burke was very reluctant to abandon an office
whose emoluments were as convenient to him as to his
spendthrift colleague. According to another and more
probable legend, it was Burke who hurried the rupture,
and stimulated Fox's jealousy of Shelburne. The Duke
of Richmond disapproved of the secession, and remained in
the government. Sheridan also disapproved, but he
sacrificed his personal conviction to loyalty to Fox.

If Burke was responsible for the break-up of the
government, then he was the instigator of a blunder that
must be pronounced not only disastrous but culpable. It
lowered the legitimate spirit of party to the nameless
spirit of faction. The dangers from which the old liberties of the realm had just emerged, have been described by
no one so forcibly as by Burke himself. No one was so
convinced as Burke that the only way of withstanding
the arbitrary and corrupting policy of the Court was to

form a strong Whig party.   No one knew better than he
the sovereign importance and the immense difficulty of
repairing the ruin of the last twelve years by a good peace.
The Rockingham or Foxite section were obviously unable
to form an effective party with serious expectation of
power, unless they had allies.   They might, no doubt,
from personal dislike to Lord Shelburne, refuse to work
under him ; but personal dislike could be no excuse for
formally and violently working against him, when his
policy was their own, and when its success was recognized
by them no less than by him as of urgent moment.   Instead of either working with the other section of their
party, or of supporting from below the gangway that
which was the policy of both sections, they sought to
return to power by coalescing with the very man whose
criminal subservience to the King's will had brought about
the catastrophe that Shelburne was repairing.   Burke
must share the blame of this famous transaction.   He
was one of the most furious assailants of the new ministry.
He poured out a fresh invective against Lord Shelburne
every day.   Cynical contemporaries laughed as they saw
him in search of more and more humiliating parallels,
ransacking all literature from the Bible and the Roman
history down to Mother Goose's tales.   His passion carried
him so far as to breed a reaction in those who listened to
him.   " I think," wrote Mason from Yorkshire, where
Burke had been on a visit to Lord Fitzwilliam in the
autumn of 1782, " that Burke's mad obloquy against
Lord Shelburne, and these insolent pamphlets in which
he must have had a hand, will do more to fix him (Shelburne) in his office than anything else."
      This result would have actually followed, for the nation
was ill pleased at the immoral alliance between the Foxites

and the man whom, if they had been true to their opinions
a thousand times repeated, they ought at that moment to
have been impeaching. The Dissenters, who had hitherto
been his enthusiastic admirers, but who are rigid above
other men in their demand of political consistency, lamented
Burke's fall in joining the Coalition, as Priestly told him
many years after, as the fall of a friend and a brother.
But Shelburne threw away the game. "His falsehoods,"
says Horace Walpole, "his flatteries, duplicity, insincerity,
arrogance, contradictions, neglect of his friends, with all
the kindred of all these faults, were the daily topics of
contempt and ridicule; and his folly shut his eyes, nor
did he perceive that so very rapid a fall must have been
owing to his own incapacity." This is the testimony of a
hostile witness. It is borne out, however, by a circumstance of striking significance. When the King recovered
the reins at the end of 1783, not only did he send for
Pitt instead of for Shelburne, but Pitt himself neither
invited Shelburne to join him, nor in any way ever
consulted him then or afterwards, though he had
been Chancellor of the Exchequer in Shelburne's own
administration.

Whatever the causes may have been, the administration fell in the spring of 1783. It was succeeded by the
memorable ministry of the Coalition, in which Fox and
Lord North divided the real power under the nominal
lead of the Duke of Portland. Members saw Lord North
squeezed up on the Treasury bench between two men who
had a year before been daily menacing him with the axe
and the block; and it was not North whom they blamed,
but Burke and Fox. Burke had returned to the Pay
Office. His first act there was unfortunate. He restored
to their position two clerks who had been suspended for

malversation, and against whom proceedings were then
pending. When attacked for this in the House, he showed
an irritation which would have carried him to gross
lengths, if Fox and Sheridan had not by main force
pulled him down into his seat by the tails of his coat.
The restoration of the clerks was an indefensible error
of judgment, and its indiscretion was heightened by the
kind of defence which Burke tried to set up. When we
wonder at Burke's exclusion from great offices, this case of
Powell and Bembridge should not be forgotten.

The decisive event in the history of the Coalition
Government was the India Bill. The Reports of the
various select committees upon Indian affairs—the most
important of them all, the ninth and eleventh, having
been drawn up by Burke himself—had shown conclusively
that the existing system of government was thoroughly
corrupt and thoroughly inadequate. It is ascertained
pretty conclusively, that the bill for replacing that system
was conceived and drawn by Burke, and that to him
belongs whatever merit or demerit it might possess. It
was Burke who infected Fox with his own ardour, and
then, as Moore justly says, the self-kindling power of
Fox's eloquence threw such fire into his defence of the
measure, that he forgot, and his hearers never found out,
that his views were not originally and spontaneously his
own. The novelty on which the great stress of discussion
was laid, was that the bill withdrew power from the Board
of Directors, and vested the government for four years in
a commission of seven persons named in the bill, and not
removable by the House.

Burke was so convinced of the incurable iniquity of the
Company, so persuaded that it was not only full of abuses,
but, as he said, one of the most corrupt and destructive

tyrannies that probably ever existed in the world, as to
be content with nothing short of the absolute depriva-
tion of its power. He avowed himself no lover of
names, and that he only contended for good government,
from whatever quarter it might come. But the idea of
good government coming from the Company, he declared
to be desperate and untenable. This intense animosity,
which, considering his long and close familiarity with the
infamies of the rule of the Company's servants, was not
unnatural, must be allowed, however, to have blinded
him to the grave objections which really existed to his
scheme. In the first place, the Bill was indisputably
inconsistent with the spirit of his revered Constitution.
For the legislature to assume the power of naming the
members of an executive body, was an extraordinary and
mischievous innovation. Then, to put patronage, which
has been estimated by a sober authority at about three
hundred thousand pounds a year, into the hands of the
House of Commons, was still more mischievous and still
less justifiable. Worst of all, from the point of view of the
projectors themselves, after a certain time the nomination
of the Commissioners would fall to the Crown, and this
might in certain contingencies increase to a most dangerous extent the ascendancy of the royal authority. If
Burke's measure had been carried, moreover, the patronage would have been transferred to a body much less
competent than the Directors to judge of the qualities
required in the fulfilment of this or that administrative
charge. Indian promotion would have followed parliamentary and party interest. In the hands of the Directors
there was at least a partial security, in their professional
knowledge, and their personal interest in the success of
their government, that places would not be given away on

irrelevant considerations. Their system, with all its faults,
insured the acquisition of a certain considerable compe-
tency in administration, before a servant reached an elevation at which he could do much harm.

Burke defended the bill (December 1, 1783) in one
of the speeches which rank only below his greatest, and it
contains two or three passages of unsurpassed energy and
impressiveness. Everybody knows the fine page about
Fox as the descendant of Henry IV. of France, and the
happy quotation from Silius Italicus. Every book of
British eloquence contains the magnificent description
of the young magistrates who undertake the government
and the spoliation of India ; how, "animated with all the
avarice of age, and all the impetuosity of youth, they roll
in one after another, wave after wave ; and there is nothing before the eyes of the natives but an endless, hope-
less prospect of new flights of birds of prey and of passage,
with appetites continually renewing for a food that is
continually wasting." How they return home laden with
spoil; "their prey is lodged in England ; and the cries
of India are given to seas and winds, to be blown about,
in every breaking up of the monsoon, over a remote
and unhearing ocean." How in India all the vices
operate by which sudden fortune is acquired ; while in
England are often displayed by the same person the virtues which dispense hereditary wealth, so that " here the
manufacturer and the husbandman will bless the just and
punctual hand that in India has torn the cloth from the
loom, or wrested the scanty portion of rice and salt from
the peasant of Bengal, or wrung from him the very opium
in which he forgot his oppression and his oppressors."

No degree of eloquence, however, could avail to repair
faults alike in structure and in tactics. The whole design

was a masterpiece of hardihood, miscalculation, and mis-
management. The combination of interests against the
bill was instant, and it was indeed formidable. The great
army of returned nabobs, of directors, of proprietors of
East India stock, rose up in all its immense force. Every
member of every corporation that enjoyed privilege by
charter, felt the attack on the Company as if it had
been a blow directed against himself. The general public
had no particular passion for purity or good government,
and the best portion of the public was disgusted with the
Coalition. The King saw his chance. With politic auda-
city he put so strong a personal pressure on the peers, that
they threw out the Bill (December, 1783). It was to
no purpose that Fox compared the lords to the Janissaries
of a Turkish Sultan, and the King's letter to Temple, to
the rescript in which Tiberius ordered the upright Sejanus
to be destroyed. Ministers were dismissed, the young
Pitt was installed in their place, and the Whigs were
ruined. As a party, they had a few months of office after
Pitt's death, but they were excluded from power for half
a century.

CHAPTER VI.

THOUGH Burke had, at a critical period of his life, definitely abandoned the career of letters, he never withdrew from close intimacy with the groups who still live for us in the pages of Boswell, as no other literary group in our history lives. Goldsmith's famous lines in *Retaliation* show how they all deplored that he should to party give up, what was meant for mankind. They often told one another that Edmund Burke was the man whose genius pointed him out as the triumphant champion of faith and sound philosophy against deism, atheism, and David Hume. They loved to see him, as Goldsmith said, wind into his subject like a serpent. Everybody felt at the Literary Club that he had no superior in knowledge, and in colloquial dialectics only one equal. Garrick was there, and of all the names of the time he is the man whom one would perhaps most willingly have seen, because the gifts which threw not only Englishmen, but Frenchmen like Diderot, and Germans like Lichtenberg, into amazement and ecstasy, are exactly those gifts which literary description can do least to reproduce. Burke was one of his strongest admirers, and there was no more zealous attendant at the closing series of performances in which the great monarch of the stage abdicated his throne. In the last pages that he

wrote, Burke refers to his ever dear friend Garrick, dead
nearly twenty years before, as the first of actors because he
was the acutest observer of nature that he had ever known.
Among men who pass for being more serious than
players, Robertson was often in London society, and he
attracted Burke by his largeness and breadth. He sent
a copy of his history of America, and Burke thanked
him with many stately compliments for having employed
philosophy to judge of manners, and from manners having
drawn new resources of philosophy. Gibbon was there,
but the bystanders felt what was too crudely expressed
by Mackintosh, that Gibbon might have been taken from
a corner of Burke's mind without ever being missed.
Though Burke and Gibbon constantly met, it is not likely
that, until the Revolution, there was much intimacy
between them, in spite of the respect which each of them
might well have had for the vast knowledge of the other.
When the *Decline and Fall* was published, Burke read it
as everybody else did ; but he told Reynolds that he disliked the style, as very affected, mere frippery and tinsel.
Sir Joshua himself was neither a man of letters nor a keen
politician ; but he was full of literary ideas and interests,
and he was among Burke's warmest and most constant
friends, following him with an admiration and reverence
that even Johnson sometimes thought excessive. The
reader of Reynolds's famous Discourses will probably share
the wonder of his contemporaries, that a man whose time
was so absorbed in the practice of his art, should have
proved himself so excellent a master in the expression of
some of its principles. Burke was commonly credited
with a large share in their composition, but the evidence
goes no further than that Reynolds used to talk them over
with him. The friendship between the pair was full and

unalloyed. What Burke admired in the great artist was
his sense and his morals, no less than his genius ; and to a
man of his fervid and excitable temper there was the most
attractive of all charms in Sir Joshua's placidity, gentleness,
evenness, and the habit, as one of his friends described it,
of being the same all the year round. When Reynolds
died in 1792, he appointed Burke one of his executors,
and left him a legacy of two thousand pounds, besides
cancelling a bond of the same amount.

Johnson, however, is the only member of that illustrious
company who can profitably be compared with Burke in
strength and impressiveness of personality, in a large sensibility at once serious and genial, in brooding care for all the
fulness of human life. This striking pair were the two
complements of a single noble and solid type, holding
tenaciously, in a century of dissolvent speculation, to the
best ideas of a society that was slowly passing. They
were powerless to hinder the inevitable transformation.
One of them did not even dimly foresee it. But both of
them help us to understand how manliness and reverence,
strength and tenderness, love of truth and pity for man,
all flourished under old institutions and old ways of thinking, into which the forces of the time were even then silently
breathing a new spirit. The friendship between Burke
and Johnson lasted as long as they lived ; and if we remember that Johnson was a strong Tory, and declared that
the first Whig was the devil, and habitually talked about
cursed Whigs and bottomless Whigs, it is an extraordinary
fact that his relations with the greatest Whig writer and
politician of his day were marked by a cordiality, respect,
and admiration that never varied nor wavered. " Burke,"
he said in a well-known passage, " is such a man that if
you met him for the first time in the street, where you

were stopped by a drove of oxen, and you and he stepped aside to take shelter but for five minutes, he'd talk to you in such a manner that, when you parted, you would say, This is an extraordinary man. He is never what we would call humdrum ; never unwilling to begin to talk, nor in haste to leave off." That Burke was as good a listener as he was a talker, Johnson never would allow. " So desirous is he to talk," he said, " that if one is talking at this end of the table, he'll talk to somebody at the other end." Johnson was far too good a critic, and too honest a man, to assent to a remark of Robertson's, that Burke had wit. " No, sir," said the sage, most truly, " he never succeeds there. 'Tis low, 'tis conceit." Wit apart, he described Burke as the only man whose common conversation corresponded to his general fame in the world ; take up whatever topic you might please, he was ready to meet you. When Burke found a seat in Parliament, Johnson said, " Now we who know Burke, know that he will be one of the first men in the country." He did not grudge that Burke should be the first man in the House of Commons, for Burke, he said, was always the first man everywhere. Once when he was ill, somebody mentioned Burke's name. Johnson cried out, " That fellow calls forth all my powers ; were I to see Burke now it would kill me."

Burke heartily returned this high appreciation. When some flatterer hinted that Johnson had taken more than his right share of the evening's talk, Burke said, " Nay, it is enough for me to have rung the bell for him." Some one else spoke of a successful imitation of Johnson's style. Burke with vehemence denied the success : the performance, he said, had the pomp, but not the force of the original ; the nodosities of the oak, but not its strength ;

110 BURKE. [CHAP.

the contortions of the sibyl, but none of the inspiration.
When Burke showed the old sage of Bolt Court over his
fine house and pleasant gardens at Beaconsfield, *Non
invideo equidem*, Johnson said, with placid good-will, *miror
magis.* They always parted in the deep and pregnant
phrase of a sage of our own day, *except in opinion not
disagreeing.* In truth the explanation of the sympathy
between them is not far to seek. We may well believe
that Johnson was tacitly alive to the essentially conservative spirit of Burke even in his most Whiggish days. And
Burke penetrated the liberality of mind in a Tory, who
called out with loud indignation that the Irish were in a
most unnatural state, for there the minority prevailed over
the majority, and the severity of the persecution exercised
by the Protestants of Ireland against the Catholics, exceeded
that of the ten historic persecutions of the Christian Church.

The parties at Beaconsfield, and the evenings at the Turk's
Head in Gerard Street, were contemporary with the famous
days at Holbach's country house at Grandval. When we
think of the reckless themes that were so recklessly discussed by Holbach, Diderot, and the rest of that indefatigable band, we feel that, as against the French philosophic
party, an English Tory like Johnson and an English Whig
like Burke would have found their own differences too
minute to be worth considering. If the group from the
Turk's Head could have been transported for an afternoon
to Grandval, perhaps Johnson would have been the less
impatient and disgusted of the two. He had the capacity
of the more genial sort of casuist for playing with subjects,
even moral subjects, with the freedom, versatility, and
ease that are proper to literature. Burke, on the contrary,
would not have failed to see, as indeed we know that he
did not fail to see, that a social pandemonium was being

prepared in this intellectual paradise of open questions, where God and a future life, marriage and the family, every dogma of religion, every prescription of morality, and all those mysteries and pieties of human life which have been sanctified by the reverence of ages, were being busily pulled to pieces, as if they had been toys in the hands of a company of sportive children. Even the *Beggar's Opera* Burke could not endure to hear praised for its wit or its music, because his mind was filled by thought of its misplaced levity, and he only saw the mischief which such a performance tended to do to society. It would be hard to defend his judgment in this particular case, but it serves to show how Burke was never content with the literary point of view, and how ready and vigilant he was for effects more profound than those of formal criticism. It is true that Johnson was sometimes not less austere in condemning a great work of art for its bad morality. The only time when he was really angry with Hannah More was on his finding that she had read *Tom Jones*—that vicious book, he called it; he hardly knew a more corrupt work. Burke's tendency towards severity of moral judgment, however, never impaired the geniality and tenderness of his relations with those whom he loved. Bennet Langton gave Boswell an affecting account of Burke's last interview with Johnson. A few days before the old man's death, Burke and four or five other friends were sitting round his bedside. " Mr. Burke said to him, ' I am afraid, sir, such a number of us may be oppressive to you.' ' No, sir,' said Johnson, ' it is not so; and I must be in a wretched state indeed, when your company is not a delight to me.' Mr. Burke, in a tremulous voice, expressive of being very tenderly affected, replied, ' My dear sir, you have always been too good to me.' Immediately

afterwards he went away.   This was the last circumstance
in the acquaintance of these two eminent men."

One of Burke's strongest political intimacies was only
less interesting and significant than his friendship with
Johnson.   William Dowdeswell had been Chancellor of
the Exchequer in the short Rockingham administration of
1765.   He had no brilliant gifts, but he had what was
then thought a profound knowledge both of the principles
and details of the administration of the national revenue.
He was industrious, steadfast, clear-headed, inexorably
upright.   "Immersed in the greatest affairs," as Burke
said in his epitaph, "he never lost the ancient, native,
genuine, English character of a country gentleman."   And
this was the character in which Burke now and always
saw not only the true political barrier against despotism
on the one hand and the rabble on the other, but the best
moral type of civic virtue.   Those who admire Burke,
but cannot share his admiration for the country gentleman, will perhaps justify him by the assumption that he
clothed his favourite with ideal qualities which ought,
even if they did not, to have belonged to that position.

In his own modest imitation and in his own humble
scale, he was a pattern of the activity in public duty, the
hospitality towards friends, the assiduous protection of
neglected worth, which ought to be among the chief
virtues of high station.   It would perhaps be doubly
unsafe to take for granted that many of our readers have
both turned over the pages of Crabbe's *Borough*, and
carried away in their minds from that moderately affecting
poem, the description of Eusebius,—

> That pious moralist, that reasoning saint!
> Can I of worth like thine, Eusebius, speak?
> The man is willing, but the muse is weak.

Eusebius is intended for Burke, and the portrait is
a literary tribute for more substantial services.
When Crabbe came up from his native Aldborough,
with three pounds and a case of surgical instruments
in his trunk, he fondly believed that a great patron
would be found to watch over his transformation
from an unsuccessful apothecary into a popular poet.
He wrote to Lord North and Lord Shelburne, but they
did not answer his letters; booksellers returned his
copious manuscripts; the three pounds gradually disappeared; the surgical instruments went to the pawnbroker's;
and the poet found himself an outcast on the world,
without a friend, without employment, and without
bread. He owed money for his lodging, and was on the
very eve of being sent to prison, when it occurred to him to
write to Burke. It was the moment (1781) when the final
struggle with Lord North was at its fiercest, and Burke
might have been absolved if, in the stress of conflict, he
had neglected a begging-letter. As it was, the manliness
and simplicity of Crabbe's application touched him. He
immediately made an appointment with the young poet,
and convinced himself of his worth. He not only relieved
Crabbe's immediate distress with a sum of money that,
as we know, came from no affluence of his own, but carried him off to Beaconsfield, installed him there as a
member of the family, and took as much pains to find a
printer for *The Library* and *The Village*, as if they had
been his own poems. In time he persuaded the Bishop
of Norwich to admit Crabbe, in spite of his want of a
regular qualification, to holy orders. He then commended
him to the notice of Lord Chancellor Thurlow. Crabbe
found the Tiger less formidable than his terrifying reputation, for Thurlow at their first interview presented him

I

with a hundred-pound note and afterwards gave him a
living. The living was of no great value, it is true; and
it was Burke who, with untiring friendship, succeeded
in procuring something like a substantial position for him,
by inducing the Duke of Rutland to make the young par-
son his chaplain. Henceforth Crabbe's career was assured,
and he never forgot to revere and bless the man to whose
generous hand he owed his deliverance.

Another of Burke's clients, of whom we hardly know
whether to say that he is more or less known to our age
than Crabbe, is Barry, a painter of disputable eminence.
The son of a seafarer at Cork, he had been introduced to Burke in Dublin in 1762, was brought over to
England by him, introduced to some kind of employment,
and finally sent, with funds provided by the Burkes, to
study art on the continent. It was characteristic of
Burke's willingness not only to supply money but, what
is a far rarer form of kindness, to take active trouble,
that he should have followed the raw student with long
and careful letters of advice upon the proper direction of
his studies. For five years Barry was maintained abroad
by the Burkes. Most unhappily for himself he was cursed
with an irritable and perverse temper, and he lacked even
the elementary arts of conduct. Burke was generous to the
end, with that difficult and uncommon kind of generosity
which moves independently of gratitude or ingratitude in
the receiver.

From his earliest days Burke had been the eager
friend of people in distress. While he was still a student
at the Temple, or a writer for the booksellers, he picked
up a curious creature in the park, in such unpromising
circumstances that he could not forbear to take him
under his instant protection. This was Joseph Emin, the

Armenian, who had come to Europe from India with
strange heroic ideas in his head as to the deliverance of his
countrymen. Burke instantly urged him to accept the few
shillings that he happened to have in his purse, and seems
to have found employment for him as a copyist, until fortune brought other openings to the singular adventurer.
For foreign visitors Burke had always a singular con-
siderateness. Two Brahmins came to England as agents
of Ragonaut Rao, and at first underwent intolerable things
rather from the ignorance than the unkindness of our
countrymen. Burke no sooner found out what was passing, than he carried them down to Beaconsfield, and as it
was summer-time he gave them for their separate use a
spacious garden-house, where they were free to prepare
their food and perform the rites as their religion pre-
scribed. Nothing was so certain to command his fervid
sympathy as strict adherence to the rules and ceremonies
of an ancient and sacred ordering.

If he never failed to perform the offices to which we are
bound by the common sympathy of men, it is satisfactory
to think that Burke in return received a measure of these
friendly services. Among those who loved him best was
Doctor Brocklesby, the tender physician who watched and
soothed the last hours of Johnson. When we remember
how Burke's soul was harassed by private cares, chagrined
by the untoward course of public events, and mortified by
neglect from friends no less than by virulent reproach from
foes, it makes us feel very kindly towards Brocklesby, to
read what he wrote to Burke in 1788 :—

My very dear friend,—
    My veneration of your public conduct for many years past,
and my real affection for your private virtues and transcendent
worth, made me yesterday take a liberty with you in a moment's

conversation at my house, to make you an instant present of
1000*l.*, which for years past I had by will destined as a testimony
of my regard on my decease. This you modestly desired me not to
think of; but I told you what I now repeat, that unfavoured as I
have lived for a long life, unnoticed professionally by any party
of men, and though unknown at court, I am rich enough to spare
to virtue (what others waste in vice) the above sum, and still
reserve an annual income greater than I spend. I shall receive
at the India House a bill I have discounted for 1000*l.* on the 4th
of next month, and then shall be happy that you will accept this
proof of my sincere love and esteem, and let me add, *Si res ampla
domi similisque affectibus esset,* I should be happy to repeat the
like every year."

The mere transcription of the friendly man's good letter
has something of the effect of an exercise of religion. And
it was only one of a series of kind acts on the part of the
same generous giver.

It is always interesting in the case of a great man to
know how he affected the women of his acquaintance.
Women do not usually judge character either so kindly or
so soundly as men do, for they lack that knowledge of the
ordeals of practical life, which gives both justice and charity
to such verdicts.   But they are more susceptible than
most men are to devotion and nobility in character.
The little group of the blue-stockings of the day regarded
the great master of knowledge and eloquence with mixed
feelings. They felt for Burke the adoring reverence which
women offer, with too indiscriminate a trust, to men of
commanding power.   In his case it was the moral lofti-
ness of his character that inspired them, as much as the
splendour of his ability.   Of Sheridan or of Fox they
could not bear to hear; of Burke they could not hear
enough.   Hannah More, and Mrs. Elizabeth Carter, the
learned translator of Epictetus, and Fanny Burney, the
author of *Evelina and Cecilia,* were all proud of his notice,

even while they glowed with anger at his sympathy with
American rebels, his unkind words about the King, and
his cruel persecution of poor Mr. Hastings.   It was at
Mrs. Vesey's evening parties, given on the Tuesdays on
which the Club dined at the Turk's Head, that he often
had long chats with Hannah More.   She had to forget
what she called his political malefactions, before she could
allow herself to admire his high spirits and good humour.
This was after the events of the Coalition, and her
Memoirs, like the change in the mind of the Dissenters towards Burke, show what a fall that act of
faction was believed to mark in his character.   When
he was rejected for Bristol, she moralized on the catastrophe by the quaint reflection, that Providence has
wisely contrived to render all its dispensations equal, by
making those talents which set one man so much above
another, of no esteem in the opinion of those who are
without them.

Miss Burney has described her flutter of spirits
when she first found herself in company with Burke
(1782).   It was at Sir Joshua's house on the top of
Richmond Hill, and she tells, with her usual effusion,
how she was impressed by Burke's noble figure and commanding air, his penetrating and sonorous voice, his
eloquent and copious language, the infinite variety and
rapidity of his discourse.   Burke had something to say on
every subject, from bits of personal gossip, up to the sweet
and melting landscape that lay in all its beauty before
their windows on the terrace.   He was playful, serious,
fantastic, wise.   When they next met, the great man com-
pleted his conquest by expressing his admiration of
Evelina.   Gibbon assured her that he had read the whole
five volumes in a day ; but Burke declared the feat was

impossible, for he had himself read it through without
interruption, and it had cost him three days. He showed
his regard for the authoress in a more substantial way than
by compliments and criticism. His last act, before going
out of office, in 1783, was to procure for Dr. Burney the
appointment of organist at the chapel of Chelsea.

We have spoken of the dislike of these excellent
women for Sheridan and Fox. In Sheridan's case Burke
did not much disagree with them. Their characters were
as unlike and as antipathetic as those of two men could
be ; and to antipathy of temperament was probably added
a kind of rivalry, which may justly have affected one of
them with an irritated humiliation. Sheridan was twenty
years younger than Burke, and did not come into Parliament until Burke had fought the prolonged battle of the
American war, and had achieved the victory of Economic
Reform. Yet Sheridan was immediately taken up by the
party, and became the intimate and counsellor of Charles
Fox, its leader, and of the Prince of Wales, its patron. That
Burke never failed to do full justice to Sheridan's brilliant
genius, or to bestow generous and unaffected praise on his
oratorical successes, there is ample evidence. He was of
far too high and veracious a nature to be capable of the
disparaging tricks of a poor jealousy. The humiliation
lay in the fact that circumstances had placed Sheridan in
a position, which made it natural for the world to measure
them with one another. Burke could no more like
Sheridan, than he could like the *Beggar's Opera.*
Sheridan had a levity, a want of depth, a laxity, and
dispersion of feeling, to which no degree of intellectual
brilliancy could reconcile a man of such profound moral
energy and social conviction as Burke.

The thought will perhaps occur to the reader that

Fox was not less lax than Sheridan, and yet for Fox Burke long had the sincerest friendship. He was dissolute, indolent, irregular, and the most insensate gambler that ever squandered fortune after fortune over the faro-table. It was his vices as much as his politics, that made George III. hate Fox as an English Catiline. How came Burke to accept a man of this character, first for his disciple, then for his friend, and next for his leader? The answer is a simple one. In spite of the disorders of his life, Fox, from the time when his acquaintance with Burke began, down to the time when it came to such disastrous end, and for long years afterwards, was to the bottom of his heart as passionate for freedom, justice, and beneficence as Burke ever was. These great ends were as real, as constant, as overmastering in Fox as they were in Burke. No man was ever more deeply imbued with the generous impulses of great statesmanship, with chivalrous courage, with the magnificent spirit of devotion to high imposing causes. These qualities we may be sure, and not his power as a debater and as a declaimer, won for him in Burke's heart the admiration which found such splendid expression in a passage, that will remain as a stock piece of declamation for long generations after it was first poured out as a sincere tribute of reverence and affection. Precisians, like Lafayette, might choose to see their patriotic hopes ruined rather than have them saved by Mirabeau, because Mirabeau was a debauchee. Burke's public morality was of stouter stuff, and he loved Fox because he knew that under the stains and blemishes that had been left by a deplorable education, was that sterling, inexhaustible ore in which noble sympathies are subtly compounded with resplendent powers.

If he was warmly attached to his political friends, Burke, at least before the Revolution, was usually on fair terms in private life with his political opponents. There were few men whose policy he disliked more than he disliked the policy of George Grenville. And we have seen that he criticized Grenville in a pamphlet which did not spare him. Yet Grenville and he did not refuse one another's hospitality, and were on the best terms to the very end. Wilberforce, again, was one of the staunchest friends of Pitt, and fought one of the greatest electioneering battles on Pitt's side in the struggle of 1784; but it made no difference in Burke's relations with him. In 1787 a coldness arose between them. Burke had delivered a strong invective against the French Treaty. Wilberforce said, "We can make allowance for the honourable gentleman, because we remember him in better days." The retort greatly nettled Burke, but the feeling soon passed away, and they both found a special satisfaction in the dinner to which Wilberforce invited Burke every session. "He was a great man," says Wilberforce. "I could never understand how at one time he grew to be so entirely neglected."

Outside of both political and literary circles, among Burke's correspondents was that wise and honest traveller whose name is as inseparably bound up with the preparation of the French Revolution, as Burke's is bound up with its sanguinary climax and fulfilment. Arthur Young, by his Farmer's Letters, and Farmer's Calendar, and his account of his travels in the southern counties of England and elsewhere—the story of the more famous travels in France was not published until 1792—had won a reputation as the best informed agriculturist of his day. Within a year of his settlement at Beaconsfield, we find Burke writing to

consult Young on the mysteries of his new occupation.
The reader may smile as he recognizes the ardour, the
earnestness, the fervid gravity of the political speeches,
in letters which discuss the merits of carrots in fattening
porkers, and the precise degree to which they should be
boiled. Burke throws himself just as eagerly into white
peas and Indian corn, into cabbages that grow into head
and cabbages that shoot into leaves, into experiments with
pumpkin seed and wild parsnip, as if they had been details of the Stamp Act, or justice to Ireland. When he
complains that it is scarcely possible for him, with his
numerous avocations, to get his servants to enter fully into
his views as to the right treatment of his crops, we can
easily understand that his farming did not help him to
make money. It is impossible that he should have had
time or attention to spare for the effectual direction of
even a small farm.

Yet if the farm brought scantier profit than it ought
to have brought, it was probably no weak solace in
the background of a life of harassing interests and perpetual disappointments. Burke was happier at Beaconsfield than anywhere else, and he was happiest there when
his house was full of guests. Nothing pleased him better
than to drive a visitor over to Windsor, where he would
expatiate with enthusiasm "on the proud Keep, rising
in the majesty of proportion, and girt with the double
belt of its kindred and coeval towers, overseeing and
guarding the subjected land." He delighted to point
out the house at Uxbridge where Charles I. had
carried on the negotiations with the Parliamentary
Commissioners; the beautiful grounds of Bulstrode,
where Judge Jefferies had once lived; and the church-
yard of Beaconsfield, where lay the remains of
Edmund Waller, the poet. He was fond of talking of

great statesmen—of Walpole, of Pulteney, and of Chatham. Some one had said that Chatham knew nothing
whatever except Spenser's *Faery Queen.* " No matter
how that was said," Burke replied to one of his visitors,
"whoever relishes and reads Spenser as he ought to be read,
will have a strong hold of the English language." The
delight of the host must have been at least equalled
by the delight of the guest in conversation which was thus
ever taking new turns, branching into topical surprises,
and at all turns and on every topic was luminous, high,
edifying, full.

No guest was more welcome than the friend of his boy-
hood, and Richard Shackleton has told how the friendship,
cordiality, and openness with which Burke embraced him
was even more than might be expected from long love.
The simple Quaker was confused by the sight of what
seemed to him so sumptuous and worldly a life, and he went
to rest uneasily, doubting whether God's blessing could go
with it. But when he awoke on the morrow of his first
visit, he told his wife, in the language of his sect, how
glad he was " to find no condemnation ; but on the contrary, ability to put up fervent petitions with much tenderness on behalf of this great luminary." It is at his country home that we like best to think of Burke. It is still
a touching picture to the historic imagination to follow
him from the heat and violence of the House, where tipsy
squires derided the greatest genius of his time, down to
the calm shades of Beaconsfield, where he would with his
own hands give food to a starving beggar, or medicine to a
peasant sick of the ague ; where he would talk of the wea-
ther, the turnips, and the hay with the team-men and the
farm-bailiff ; and where, in the evening stillness, he would
pace the walk under the trees, and reflect on the state of
Europe and the distractions of his country.

CHAPTER VII.

THE six years which followed the destruction of the Coalition were, in some respects, the most mortifying portion of Burke's troubled career. Pitt was more firmly seated in power than Lord North had ever been, and he used his power to carry out a policy against which it was impossible for the Whigs, on their own principles, to offer an effective resistance. For this is the peculiarity of the King's first victory over the enemies who had done obstinate battle with him for nearly a quarter of a century. He had driven them out of the field, but with the aid of an ally who was as strongly hostile to the royal system as they had ever been. The King had vindicated his right against the Whigs to choose his own ministers; but the new minister was himself a Whig by descent, and a reformer by his education and personal disposition.

Ireland was the subject of the first great battle between the ministry and their opponents. Here, if anywhere, we might have expected from Burke at least his usual wisdom and patience. We saw in a previous chapter (p. 23) what the political condition of Ireland was, when Burke went there with Hamilton in 1763. The American war had brought about a great change.

The King had shrewdly predicted that if America became free, Ireland would soon follow the same plan and
be a separate state. In fact, along with the American
war we had to encounter an Irish war also; but the
latter was, as an Irish politician called it at the time, a
smothered war. Like the Americans, the Anglo-Irish
entered into non-importation compacts, and they inter-
dicted commerce. The Irish volunteers, first forty, then
sixty, and at last a hundred thousand strong, were virtually an army enrolled to overawe the English ministry
and Parliament. Following the spirit, if not the actual
path, of the Americans, they raised a cry for commercial
and legislative independence. They were too strong to
be resisted, and in 1782 the Irish Parliament acquired
the privilege of initiating and conducting its own business,
without the sanction or control either of the Privy Council
or of the English Parliament. Dazzled by the chance of
acquiring legislative independence, they had been content
with the comparatively small commercial boons obtained
by Lord Nugent and Burke in 1778, and with the removal
of further restrictions by the alarmed minister in the following year. After the concession of their independence
in 1782, they found that to procure the abolition of the
remaining restrictions on their commerce—the right of
trade, for instance, with America and Africa—the consent of the English legislature was as necessary as it had
ever been. Pitt, fresh from the teaching of Adam Smith
and of Shelburne, brought forward in 1785 his famous
commercial propositions. The theory of his scheme was
that Irish trade should be free, and that Ireland should be
admitted to a permanent participation in commercial advantages. In return for this gain, after her hereditary
revenue passed a certain point, she was to devote the sur-

plus to purposes, such as the maintenance of the navy, in which the two nations had a common interest. Pitt was to be believed when he declared that of all the objects of his political life this was, in his opinion, the most important that he had ever engaged in, and he never expected to meet another that should rouse every emotion in so strong a degree as this.

A furious battle took place in the Irish Parliament. There, while nobody could deny that the eleven propositions would benefit the mercantile interests of the country, it was passionately urged that the last of the propositions, that which concerned the apportionment of Irish revenue to imperial purposes, meant the enslavement of their unhappy island. Their fetters, they went on, were clenched, if the English Government was to be allowed thus to take the initiative in Irish legislation. The factious course pursued by the English Opposition was much less excusable than the line of the Anglo-Irish leaders. Fox, who was ostentatiously ignorant of political economy, led the charge. He insisted that Pitt's measures would annihilate English trade, would destroy the Navigation Laws, and with them would bring our maritime strength to the ground. Having thus won the favour of the English manufacturers, he turned round to the Irish Opposition, and conciliated them by declaring with equal vehemence that the propositions were an insult to Ireland, and a nefarious attempt to tamper with her new-born liberties. Burke followed his leader. We may almost say that for once he allowed his political integrity to be bewildered. In 1778 and 1779 he had firmly resisted the pressure which his mercantile constituents in Bristol had endeavoured to put upon him; he had warmly supported the Irish claims, and had lost his seat in con-

sequence. The precise ground which he took up in 1785
was this. He appears to have discerned in Pitt's proposals
the germ of an attempt to extract revenue from Ireland,
identical in purpose, principle, and probable effect with
the ever-memorable attempt to extract revenue from the
American Colonies. Whatever stress may be laid upon
this, we find it hard to vindicate Burke from the charge
of factiousness. Nothing can have been more unworthy
of him than the sneer at Pitt in the great speech on the
Nabob of Arcot's debts (1785), for stopping to pick up
chaff and straws from the Irish revenue, instead of check-
ing profligate expenditure in India.

Pitt's alternative was irresistible. Situated as Ireland
was, she must either be the subservient instrument of
English prosperity, or else she must be allowed to enjoy
the benefits of English trade, taking at the same time
a proportionate share of the common burdens. Adam
Smith had shown that there was nothing incompatible with
justice in a contribution by Ireland to the public debt of
of Great Britain. That debt, he argued, had been con-
tracted in support of the government established by the
Revolution ; a government to which the Protestants of
Ireland owed not only the whole authority which they
enjoyed in their own country, but every security which
they possessed for their liberty, property, and religion.
The neighbourhood of Ireland to the shores of the mother
country introduced an element into the problem, which must
have taught every unimpassioned observer that the American
solution would be inadequate for a dependency that lay
at our very door. Burke could not, in his calmer moments,
have failed to recognize all this. Yet he lent himself to the
party cry that Pitt was taking his first measures for the re-
enslavement of Ireland. Had it not been for what he him-

self called the delirium of the preceding session, and which had still not subsided, he would have seen that Pitt was in truth taking his first measures for the effective deliverance of Ireland from an unjust and oppressive subordination. The same delirium committed him to another equally deplorable perversity, when he opposed, with as many excesses in temper as fallacies in statesmanship, the wise treaty with France, in which Pitt partially anticipated the commercial policy of an ampler treaty three-quarters of a century afterwards.

A great episode in Burke's career now opened. It was in 1785 that Warren Hastings returned from India, after a series of exploits as momentous and far-reaching, for good or evil, as have ever been achieved by any English ruler. For years Burke had been watching India. With rising wonder, amazement, and indignation he had steadily followed that long train of intrigue and crime which had ended in the consolidation of a new empire. With the return of Hastings he felt that the time had come for striking a severe blow, and making a signal example. He gave notice (June, 1785) that he would, at a future day, make a motion respecting the conduct of a gentleman just returned from India.

Among minor considerations, we have to remember that Indian affairs entered materially into the great battle of parties. It was upon an Indian bill that the late ministry had made shipwreck. It was notoriously by the aid of potent Indian interests that the new ministry had acquired a portion of its majority. To expose the misdeeds of our agents in India was at once to strike the minister who had dexterously secured their support, and to attack one of the great strongholds of parliamentary corruption. The proceedings against Hastings were, in the

first instance, regarded as a sequel to the struggle over
Fox's East India Bill. That these considerations were
present in Burke's thought there is no doubt, but they
were purely secondary. It was India itself that stood
above all else in his imagination. It had filled his mind
and absorbed his time while Pitt was still an under-
graduate at Cambridge, and Burke was looking forward
to match his plan of economic reform with a greater plan
of Indian reform. In the Ninth Report, the Eleventh
Report, and in his speech on the India Bill of 1783, he
had shown both how thoroughly he had mastered the
facts, and how profoundly they had stirred his sense of
wrong. The masterpiece known as the Speech on the
Nabob of Arcot's debts, delivered in Parliament on a
motion for papers (1785), handles matters of account, of
interest turned into principal, and principal superadded
to principal ; it deals with a hundred minute technicalities
of teeps and tuncaws, of gomastahs and soucaring ; all
with such a suffusion of interest and colour, with such
nobility of idea and expression, as could only have come
from the addition to genius of a deep morality of nature,
and an overwhelming force of conviction. A space less
than one of these pages contains such a picture of the
devastation of the Carnatic by Hyder Ali, as may fill the
young orator or the young writer with the same emotions
of enthusiasm, emulation, and despair that torment the
artist who first gazes on the Madonna at Dresden, or the
figures of Night and Dawn and the Penseroso at Florence.
The despair is only too well founded. No conscious study
could pierce the secret of that just and pathetic transition
from the havoc of Hyder Ali to the healing duties of a
virtuous government, to the consolatory celebration of the
mysteries of justice and humanity, to the warning to the

unlawful creditors to silence their inauspicious tongues in presence of the holy work of restoration, to the generous proclamation against them that in every country the first creditor is the plough. The emotions which make the hidden force of such pictures come not by observation. They grow from the sedulous meditation of long years, directed by a powerful intellect and inspired by an interest in human well-being, which of its own virtue bore the orator into the sustaining air of the upper gods. Concentrated passion and exhaustive knowledge have never entered into a more formidable combination. Yet, when Burke made his speech on the Nabob of Arcot's debts, Pitt and Grenville consulted together whether it was worth answering, and came to the conclusion that they need not take the trouble.

Neither the scornful neglect of his opponents, nor the dissuasions of some who sat on his own side, could check the ardour with which Burke pressed on, as he said, to the relief of afflicted nations. The fact is, that Burke was not at all a philanthropist as Clarkson and Wilberforce were philanthropists. His sympathy was too strongly under the control of true political reason. In 1780, for instance, the slave-trade had attracted his attention, and he had even proceeded to sketch out a code of regulations which provided for its immediate mitigation and ultimate suppression. After mature consideration he abandoned the attempt, from the conviction that the strength of the West India interest would defeat the utmost efforts of his party. And he was quite right in refusing to hope from any political action, what could only be effected after the moral preparation of the bulk of the nation. And *direct* moral or philanthropic apostleship was not his function.

Macaulay, in a famous passage of dazzling lustre and

K

fine historic colour, describes Burke's holy rage against
the misdeeds of Hastings, as due to his sensibility. But
sensibility to what ? Not merely to those common impressions of human suffering which kindle the flame of
ordinary philanthropy, always attractive, often so beneficent, but often so capricious and so laden with secret
detriment. This was no part of Burke's type. Nor is it
enough to say that Burke had what is the distinctive
mark of the true statesman, a passion for good, wise, and
orderly government. He had that in the strongest degree.
All that wore the look of confusion he held in abhorrence, and he detected the seeds of confusion with a pene-
tration that made other men marvel. He was far too wise
a man to have any sympathy with the energetic exercise of
power for power's sake. He knew well that triumphs of
violence are for the most part little better than temporary
makeshifts, which leave all the work of government to be
encountered afterwards by men of essentially greater
capacity than the hero of force without scruple. But he
regarded those whom he called the great bad men of the
old stamp, Cromwell, Richelieu, the Guises, the Condés,
with a certain tolerance, because " though the virtues of
such men were not to be taken as a balance to their
crimes, yet they had long views, and sanctified their
ambition by aiming at the orderly rule, and not the
destruction of their country." What he valued was the
deep-seated order of systems that worked by the accepted
uses, opinions, beliefs, prejudices of a community.

This love of right and stable order was not all. That
was itself the growth from a deeper root, partly of conviction and partly of sympathy; the conviction of the
rare and difficult conjunctures of circumstance which
are needed for the formation of even the rudest forms

of social union among mankind ; and then the sympathy
that the best men must always find it hard to withhold
from any hoary fabric of belief, and any venerated system
of government, that has cherished a certain order, and
shed even a ray of the faintest dawn, among the violences
and the darkness of the race. It was reverence rather
than sensibility, a noble and philosophic conservatism rather
than philanthropy, which raised that storm in Burke's
breast against the rapacity of English adventurers in India,
and the imperial crimes of Hastings. Exactly the same tide
of emotion which afterwards filled to the brim the cup
of prophetic anger against the desecrators of the church
and the monarchy of France, now poured itself out against
those who in India had " tossed about, subverted and tore
to pieces, as if it were in the gambols of boyish unlucki-
ness and malice, the most established rights, and the most
ancient and most revered institutions of ages and nations."
From beginning to end of the fourteen years in which Burke
pursued his campaign against Hastings, we see in every
page that the India which ever glowed before his vision, was
not the home of picturesque usages and melodramatic
costume, but rather, in his own words, the land of princes
once of great dignity, authority and opulence; of an ancient
and venerable priesthood, the guides of the people while
living, and their consolation in death; of a nobility of antiquity and renown; of millions of ingenious mechanics, and
millions of diligent tillers of the earth ; and finally, the land
where might be found almost all the religions professed by
men, the Brahminical, the Mussulman, the Eastern and the
Western Christian. When he published his speech on
the Nabob of Arcot, Burke prefixed to it an admirable
quotation from one of the letters of the Emperor Julian.
And Julian too, as we all know, had a strong feeling for

the past. But what in that remarkable figure was only
the sentimentalism of reaction, in Burke was a reasoned
and philosophic veneration for all old and settled order,
whether in the free Parliament of Great Britain, in the
ancient absolutism of Versailles, or in the secular pomp
of Oude, and the inviolable sanctity of Benares, the holy
city and the garden of God.

It would be out of place here to attempt to follow the
details of the impeachment. Every reader has heard that
great tale in our history, and everybody knows that it was
Burke's tenacity and power which caused that tale to be
told. The House of Commons would not, it is true, have
directed that Hastings should be impeached, unless Pitt
had given his sanction and approval, and how it was that
Pitt did give his sanction and approval so suddenly and
on grounds ostensibly so slender, remains one of the secrets
of history. In no case would the impeachment have been
pressed upon Parliament by the Opposition, and assented
to by ministers, if Burke had not been there with his pro-
digious industry, his commanding comprehensive vision,
his burning zeal, and his power of kindling in men so
different from him and from one another as Fox, Sheridan,
Windham, Grey, a zeal only less intense than his own.

It was in the spring of 1786 that the articles of charge
of Hastings's high crimes and misdemeanours, as Burke
had drawn them, were presented to the House of Commons. It was in February, 1788, that Burke opened the
vast cause in the old historic hall at Westminster, in an
oration in which at points he was wound up to such a pitch
of eloquence and passion that every listener, including the
great criminal, held his breath in an agony of horror; that
women were carried out fainting; that the speaker himself
became incapable of saying another word, and the specta-

tors of the scene began to wonder whether he would not, like the mighty Chatham, actually die in the exertion of his overwhelming powers. Among the illustrious crowd who thronged Westminster Hall in the opening days of the impeachment, was Fanny Burney. She was then in her odious bondage at Court, and was animated by that admiration and pity for Hastings which at Court was the fashion. Windham used to come up from the box of the managers of the impeachment to talk over with her the incidents of the day, and she gave him her impressions of Burke's speech, which were probably those of the majority of his hearers, for the majority were favourable to Hastings. " I told him," says Miss Burney, "that Mr. Burke's opening had struck me with the highest admiration of his powers, from the eloquence, the imagination, the fire, the diversity of expression, and the ready flow of language with which he seemed gifted, in a most superior manner, for any and every purpose to which rhetoric could lead." " And when he came to his two narratives," I continued, " when he related the particulars of those dreadful murders, he interested, he engaged, he at last overpowered me ; I felt my cause lost. I could hardly keep on my seat. My eyes dreaded a single glance towards a man so accused as Mr. Hastings ; I wanted to sink on the floor, that they might be saved so painful a sight. I had no hope he could clear himself ; not another wish in his favour remained. But when from this narration Mr. Burke proceeded to his own comments and declamation— when the charges of rapacity, cruelty, tyranny, were general, and made with all the violence of personal detestation, and continued and aggravated without any further fact or illustration ; then there appeared more of study than of truth, more of invective than of justice ; and,

in short, so little of proof to so much of passion, that
in a very short time I began to lift up my head, my
seat was no longer uneasy, my eyes were indifferent
which way they looked, or what object caught them,
and before I was myself aware of the declension of Mr.
Burke's powers over my feelings, I found myself a mere
spectator in a public place, and looking all around it, with
my opera-glass in my hand !"

In 1795, six years after Burke's opening, the Lords were
ready with their verdict. It had long been anticipated.
Hastings was acquitted. This was the close of the fourteen
years of labour, from the date of the Select Committee of
1781. " If I were to call for a reward," Burke said, " it
would be for the services in which for fourteen years,
without intermission, I showed the most industry and had
the least success. I mean the affairs of India ; they are
those on which I value myself the most ; most for the
importance ; most for the labour ; most for the judgment ;
most for constancy and perseverance in the pursuit."

The side that is defeated on a particular issue, is often
victorious in the wide and general outcome. Looking
back across the ninety years that divide us from that
memorable scene in Westminster Hall, we may see that
Burke had more success than at first appeared. If he did
not convict the man, he overthrew a system, and stamped
its principles with lasting censure and shame. Burke had
perhaps a silent conviction that it would have been better
for us and for India, if Clive had succeeded in his attempt
to blow out his own brains in the Madras counting-house,
or if the battle of Plassy had been a decisive defeat instead
of a decisive victory. " All these circumstances," he once
said, in reference to the results of the investigation of the
Select Committee, " are not, I confess, very favourable to

the idea of our attempting to govern India at all. But
there we are : there we are placed by the Sovereign Dis-
poser, and we must do the best we can in our situation.
The situation of man is the preceptor of his duty." If that
situation is better understood now than it was a century
ago, and that duty more loftily conceived, the result is
due, so far as such results can ever be due to one man's
action apart from the confluence of the deep impersonal
elements of time, to the seeds of justice and humanity
which were sown by Burke and his associates. Nobody
now believes that Clive was justified in tricking Omichund
by forging another man's name ; that Impey was justified
in hanging Nuncomar for committing the very offence for
which Clive was excused or applauded, although forgery is
no grave crime according to Hindoo usage, and it is the
gravest according to English usage ; that Hastings did
well in selling English troops to assist in the extermina-
tion of a brave people with whom he was at peace ; that
Benfield did well in conniving with an Eastern prince in
a project of extortion against his subjects. The whole
drift of opinion has changed, and it is since the trial of
Hastings that the change has taken place. The question
in Burke's time was whether oppression and corruption
were to continue to be the guiding maxims of English
policy. The personal disinterestedness of the ruler who
had been the chief founder of this policy, and had most
openly set aside all pretence of righteous principle, was
dust in the balance. It was impossible to suppress the
policy without striking a deadly blow at its most eminent
and powerful instrument. That Hastings was acquitted,
was immaterial. The lesson of his impeachment had been
taught with sufficiently impressive force—the great lesson
that Asiatics have rights, and that Europeans have obli-

gations ; that a superior race is bound to observe the
highest current morality of the time in all its dealings
with the subject race. Burke is entitled to our lasting
reverence as the first apostle and great upholder of integrity,
mercy, and honour in the relation between his countrymen
and their humble dependents.

He shared the common fate of those who dare to
strike a blow for human justice against the prejudices of
national egotism. But he was no longer able to bear obloquy
and neglect, as he had borne it through the war with the
colonies. When he opened the impeachment of Hastings
at Westminster, Burke was very near to his sixtieth year.
Hannah More noted in 1786 that his vivacity had diminished, and that business and politics had impaired his
agreeableness. The simpletons in the House, now that they
had at last found in Pitt a political chief who could beat
the Whig leaders on their own ground of eloquence, knowledge, and dexterity in debate, took heart as they had
never done under Lord North. They now made deliberate
attempts to silence the veteran by unmannerly and brutal
interruptions, of which a mob of lower class might have
been ashamed. Then suddenly came a moment of such
excitement as has not often been seen in the annals of
party. It became known one day in the autumn of 1788,
that the King had gone out of his mind.

The news naturally caused the liveliest agitation among
the Whigs. When the severity of the attack forced the
ministry to make preparations for a Regency, the friends
of the Prince of Wales assumed that they would speedily
return to power, and hastened to form their plans accordingly. Fox was travelling in Italy with Mrs. Armitage, and
he had been two months away without hearing a word from
England. The Duke of Portland sent a messenger in search

of him, and after a journey of ten days the messenger
found him at Bologna. Fox instantly set off in all haste
for London, which he reached in nine days. The three
months that followed were a time of unsurpassed activity
and bitterness, and Burke was at least as active and as
bitter as the rest of them. He was the writer of the
Prince of Wales's letter to Pitt, sometimes set down to
Sheridan, and sometimes to Gilbert Elliot. It makes us
feel how naturally the style of ideal kingship, its dignity,
calm, and high self-consciousness all came to Burke.
Although we read of his thus drawing up manifestoes and
protests, and deciding minor questions for Fox, which Fox
was too irresolute to decide for himself, yet we have it on
Burke's own authority that some time elapsed after the
return to England before he even saw Fox ; that he was not
consulted as to the course to be pursued in the grave and
difficult questions connected with the Regency ; and that
he knew as little of the inside of Carlton House, where
the Prince of Wales lived, as of Buckingham House, where
the King lived. " I mean to continue here," he says to
Charles Fox, " until you call upon me ; and I find myself
perfectly easy, from the implicit confidence that I have in
you and the Duke, and the certainty that I am in that you
two will do the best for the general advantage of the cause.
In that state of mind I feel no desire whatsoever of inter-
fering." Yet the letter itself, and others which follow,
testify to the vehemence of Burke's interest in the matter,
and to the persistency with which he would have had
them follow his judgment, if they would have listened.
It is as clear that they did not listen.

Apart from the fierce struggle against Pitt's Regency
Bill, Burke's friends were intently occupied with the
reconstruction of the Portland cabinet, which the king

had so unexpectedly dismissed five years before. This
was a sphere in which Burke's gifts were neither required
nor sought. We are rather in distress, Sir Gilbert
Elliot writes, for a proper man for the office of Chancellor of the Exchequer. "Lord J. Cavendish is very
unwilling to engage again in public affairs. Fox is to be
Secretary of State. Burke, it is thought, would not be
approved of, Sheridan has not the public confidence, and
so it comes down therefore to Grey, Pelham, myself, and
perhaps Windham." Elliot was one of Burke's most
faithful and attached friends, and he was intimately concerned in all that was going on in the inner circle of the
party. It is worth while, therefore, to reproduce his
account from a confidential letter to Lady Elliot, of the
way in which Burke's claim to recognition was at this
time regarded and dealt with.

Although I can tell you nothing positive about my own situation, I was made very happy indeed yesterday by co-operating in
the settlement of Burke's, in a manner which gives us great joy as
well as comfort. The Duke of Portland has felt distressed how
to arrange Burke and his family in a manner equal to Burke's
merits, and to the Duke's own wishes, and at the same time so as
to be exempt from the many difficulties which seem to be in the
way. He sent for Pelham and me, as Burke's friends and his
own, to advise with us about it; and we dined yesterday with
him and the Duchess, that we might have time to talk the thing
over at leisure and without interruption after dinner. We stayed
accordingly, engaged in that subject till almost twelve at night,
and our conference ended most happily, and excessively to the
satisfaction of us all. The Duke of Portland has the veneration
for Burke that Windham, Pelham, myself and a few more have,
and he thinks it impossible to do too much for him. He considers
the reward to be given to Burke as a credit and honour to the
nation, and he considers the neglect of him and his embarrassed
situation as having been long a reproach to the country. The
unjust prejudice and clamour which has prevailed against him
and his family only determine the Duke the more to do him

justice. The question was how? First, his brother Richard,
who was Secretary to the Treasury before, will have the same
office now, but the Duke intends to give him one of the first
offices which falls vacant, of about 1000*l.* a year for life in the
Customs, and he will then resign the Secretary to the Treasury,
which, however, in the meanwhile is worth 3000*l.* a year. Edmund
Burke is to have the Pay Office, 4000*l.* a year; but as that is pre-
carious and he can leave no provision for his son, it would, in fact, be
doing little or nothing of any real or substantial value unless
some *permanent* provision is added to it. In this view the Duke
is to grant him on the Irish establishment a pension of 2000*l.* a
year *clear* for his own life, and the other half to Mrs. Burke for
her life. This will make Burke completely happy, by leaving his
wife and son safe from want after his death, if they should survive
him. The Duke's affectionate anxiety to accomplish this object,
and his determination to set all clamour at defiance on this point
of justice, was truly affecting, and increases my attachment for
the Duke. . . . The Duke said the only objection to this plan
was that he thought it was due from this country, and that he
grudged the honour of it to Ireland; but as nothing in England
was ready, this plan was settled. You may think it strange that
to this moment Burke does not know a word of all this, and his
family are indeed, I believe, suffering a little under the apprehension that he may be neglected in the general scramble. I believe
there never were three cabinet counsellors more in harmony
on any subject than we were, nor three people happier in their
day's work.[3]

This leaves the apparent puzzle where it was. Why
should Burke not be approved of for Chancellor of the
Exchequer? What were the many difficulties described
as seeming to be in the way of arranging for Burke, in a
manner equal to Burke's merits and the Duke of Portland's wishes? His personal relations with the chiefs
of his party were at this time extremely cordial and
intimate. He was constantly a guest at the Duke of
Portland's most private dinner-parties. Fox had gone
down to Beaconsfield to recruit himself from the fatigues

[3] *Life and Letters of Sir G. Elliot,* i. 261-3.

of his rapid journey from Bologna, and to spend some days
in quiet with Windham and the master of the house.
Elliot and Windham, who were talked about for a post
for which one of them says that Burke would not have
been approved, vied with one another in adoring Burke.
Finally, Elliot and the Duke think themselves happy in a
day's work, which ended in consigning the man who not
only was, but was admitted to be, the most powerful genius
of their party, to a third-rate post, and that most equivocal
distinction, a pension on the Irish establishment. The
common explanation that it illustrates Whig exclusiveness,
cannot be seriously received as adequate. It is probable,
for one thing, that the feelings of the Prince of Wales had
more to do with it, than the feelings of men like the Duke
of Portland or Fox. We can easily imagine how little
that most worthless of human creatures would appreciate
the great qualities of such a man as Burke. The painful
fact which we are unable to conceal from ourselves is,
that the common opinion of better men than the Prince of
Wales leaned in the same direction. His violence in the
course of the Regency debates had produced strong disapproval in the public, and downright consternation in
his own party. On one occasion he is described by a
respectable observer as having " been wilder than ever,
and laid himself and his party more open than ever
speaker did. He is folly personified, but shaking his cap
and bells under the laurel of genius. He finished his
wild speech in a manner next to madness." Moore believes that Burke's indiscretions in these trying and prolonged transactions sowed the seeds of the alienation
between him and Fox two years afterwards. Burke's
excited state of mind showed itself in small things as well
as great. Going with Windham to Carlton House, Burke

attacked him in the coach for a difference of opinion about
the affairs of a friend, and behaved with such unreasonable
passion and such furious rudeness of manner, that his
magnanimous admirer had some difficulty in obliterating
the impression. The public were less tolerant. Windham
has told us that at this time Burke was a man decried,
persecuted, and proscribed, not being much valued even
by his own party, and by half the nation considered as
little better than an ingenious madman.[4] This is evidence
beyond impeachment, for Windham loved and honoured
Burke with the affection and reverence of a son; and he
puts the popular sentiment on record with grief and amazement. There is other testimony to the same effect. The
late Lord Lansdowne, who must have heard the subject
abundantly discussed by those who were most concerned
in it, was once asked by a very eminent man of our own
time, why the Whigs kept Burke out of their cabinets.
" Burke !" he cried ; " he was so violent, so overbearing,
so arrogant, so intractable, that to have got on with
him in a cabinet would have been utterly and absolutely
impossible."

On the whole, it seems to be tolerably clear that the
difficulties in the way of Burke's promotion to high office
were his notoriously straitened circumstances; his un-
governed excesses of party zeal and political passion;
finally, what Sir Gilbert Elliot calls the unjust prejudice
and clamour against him and his family, and what Burke
himself once called the hunt of obloquy that pursued him
all his life. The first two of these causes can scarcely have
operated in the arrangements that were made in the Rockingham and Coalition ministries. But the third, we may
be sure, was incessantly at work. It would have needed

4 Windham's *Diary*, p. 213.

social courage alike in 1782, 1783, and 1788 to give cabinet
rank to a man round whose name there floated so many disparaging associations. Social courage is exactly the virtue
in which the constructors of a government will always
think themselves least able to indulge. Burke, we have to
remember, did not stand alone before the world. Elliot
describes a dinner-party at Lord Fitzwilliams's, at which
four of these half-discredited Irishmen were present.
" Burke has now got such a train after him as would sink
anybody but himself:—his son, who is quite *nauseated* by
all mankind ; his brother, who is liked better than his
son, but is rather offensive with animal spirits and with
brogue ; and his cousin, Will Burke, who is just returned
unexpectedly from India, as much ruined as when he
went many years ago, and who is a fresh charge on any
prospects of power that Burke may ever have." It was
this train, and the ideas of adventurership that clung to
them, the inextinguishable stories about papistry and Saint
Omer's, the tenacious calumny about the letters of Junius,
the notorious circumstances of embarrassment and neediness—it was all these things which combined with Burke's
own defects of temper and discretion, to give the Whig
grandees as decent a reason as they could have desired for
keeping all the great posts of state in their own hands.

It seems difficult to deny that the questions of the Regency had caused the germs of a sort of dissatisfaction
and strain in the relations between Fox and Burke. Their
feelings to one another have been well compared to the
mutual discontent between partners in unsuccessful play,
where each suspects that it is the mistakes of the other that
lost the game. Whether Burke felt conscious of the failures
in discretion and temper, which were the real or pretended
excuse for neglect, we cannot tell. There is one passage

that reveals a chagrin of this kind. A few days after the
meeting between the Duke of Portland and Elliot, for the
purpose of settling his place in the new ministry, Burke
went down to Beaconsfield. In writing (January 24th,
1789) to invite Windham and Pelham to come to stay
a night, with promise of a leg of mutton cooked by a
dairy-maid who was not a bad hand at a pinch, he goes on
to say that his health has received some small benefit from
his journey to the country. "But this view to health,
though far from unnecessary to me, was not the chief
cause of my present retreat. I began to find that I
was grown rather too anxious ; and had begun to discover to myself and to others a solicitude relative to
the present state of affairs, which, though their strange
condition might well warrant it in others, is certainly less
suitable to my time of life, in which all emotions are less
allowed ; and to which, most certainly, all human concerns
ought in reason to become more indifferent, than to those
who have work to do, and a good deal of day, and of inex-
hausted strength to do it in." [5]

The King's unexpected restoration to health two or three
weeks later, brought to nought all the hope and ambition
of the Whigs, and confirmed Pitt in power for the rest of
Burke's lifetime. But an event now came to pass in
the world's history, which transformed Burke in an instant from a man decried, persecuted, proscribed, into an
object of exultant adoration all over Europe.

[5] *Correspondence*, iii. 89.

CHAPTER VIII.

WE have now come to the second of the two momentous changes in the world's affairs, in which Burke played
an imposing and historic part. His attitude in the first
of them, the struggle for American independence, com-
mands almost without alloy the admiration and reverence
of posterity. His attitude in the second of them, the
great revolution in France, has raised controversies which
can only be compared in heat and duration to the master
controversies of theology. If the history of society were
written as learned men write the history of the Christian
faith and its churches, Burke would figure in the same strong
prominence whether deplorable or glorious, as Arius and
Athanasius, Augustine and Sabellius, Luther and Ignatius.
If we ask how it is that now, nearly a century after the event,
men are still discussing Burke's pamphlet on the Revolution
as they are still discussing Bishop Butler's *Analogy*, the
answer is that in one case as in the other the questions at
issue are still unsettled, and that Burke offers in their
highest and most comprehensive form all the considerations that belong to one side of the dispute. He was not
of those, of whom Coleridge said that they proceeded with
much solemnity to solve the riddle of the French Revolution by anecdotes. He suspended it in the same light

of great social ideas and wide principles, in which its authors and champions professed to represent it. Unhappily he advanced from criticism to practical exhortation, in our opinion the most mischievous and indefensible that has ever been pressed by any statesman on any nation. But the force of the criticism remains, its foresight remains, its commemoration of valuable elements of life which men were forgetting, its discernment of the limitations of things, its sense of the awful emergencies of the problem. When our grandchildren have made up their minds, once for all, as to the merits of the social transformation which dawned on Europe in 1789, then Burke's *Reflections* will become a mere literary antiquity, and not before.

From the very beginning Burke looked upon the proceedings in France with distrust. He had not a moment of enthusiasm or sympathy of which to repent. When the news reached England that the insurgents of Paris had stormed the Bastille, Fox exclaimed with exultation, how much it was the greatest event that had ever happened in the world, how much the best. Is it an infirmity to wish, for an instant, that some such phrase of generous hope had escaped from Burke ; that he had for a day or an hour undergone that fine illusion which was lighted up in the spirits of men like Wordsworth and Coleridge ? Those great poets, who were destined one day to preach even a wiser and a loftier conservatism than his own, have told us what they felt—

> When France in wrath her giant limbs upreared,
> And with that oath, which smote air, earth, and sea,
> Stamped her strong foot, and said she would be free.

Burke from the first espied the looming shadow of a catastrophe. In August he wrote to Lord Charlemont

L

that the events in France had something paradoxical and
mysterious about them; that the outbreak of the old
Parisian ferocity might be no more than a sudden explo-
sion, but if it should happen to be *character* rather than
accident, then the people would need a strong hand like
that of their former masters to coerce them; that all
depended upon the French having wise heads among
them, and upon these wise heads, if such there were,
acquiring an authority to match their wisdom.   There is
nothing here but a calm and sagacious suspense of judgment.   It soon appeared that the old Parisian ferocity was
still alive.   In the events of October, 1789, when the
mob of Paris marched out to Versailles and marched back
again with the King and Queen in triumphal procession,
Burke felt in his heart that the beginning of the end had
come, and that the catastrophe was already at hand.   In
October he wrote a long letter to the French gentleman
to whom he afterwards addressed the *Reflections*.   "You
hope, sir," he said, "that I think the French deserving of
liberty.   I certainly do.   I certainly think that all men
who desire it deserve it.   We cannot forfeit our right
to it, but by what forfeits our title to the privileges of
our kind.   The liberty I mean is *social* freedom.   It is
that state of things in which liberty is secured by equality
of restraint.   This kind of liberty is, indeed, but another
name for justice.   *Whenever a separation is made between liberty and justice, neither is in my opinion safe.*"
The weightiest and most important of all political truths,
and worth half the fine things that poets have sung about
freedom—if it could only have been respected, how
different the course of the Revolution !   But the engineer
who attempts to deal with the abysmal rush of the falls
of Niagara, must put aside the tools that constructed the

Bridgewater Canal and the Chelsea Waterworks. No-body recognised so early as Burke that France had really embarked among cataracts and boiling gulfs, and the pith of all his first criticisms, including the *Reflections*, was the proposition that to separate freedom from justice was nothing else than to steer the ship of state direct into the Maelstrom. It is impossible to deny that this was true. Unfortunately it was a truth which the wild spirits that were then abroad in the storm made of no avail.

Destiny aimed an evil stroke when Burke, whose whole soul was bound up in order, peace, and gently enlarged precedent, found himself face to face with the portentous man-devouring Sphinx. He, who could not endure that a few clergymen should be allowed to sub-scribe to the Bible instead of to the Articles, saw the ancient Church of Christendom prostrated, its possessions confiscated, its priests proscribed, and Christianity itself officially superseded. The economical reformer, who when his zeal was hottest declined to discharge a tide-waiter or a scullion in the royal kitchen, who should have acquired the shadow of a vested interest in his post, beheld two great orders stripped of their privileges and deprived of much of their lands, though their possession had been sanctified by the express voice of the laws and the prescription of many centuries. He, who was full of apprehension and anger at the proposal to take away a member of Parliament from St. Michael's or Old Sarum, had to look on while the most august monarchy in Europe was overturned. The man who dreaded fanatics, hated atheists, despised political theorisers, and was driven wild at the notion of applying metaphysical rights and abstract doctrines to public affairs, sud-denly beheld a whole kingdom given finally up to

fanatics, atheists, and theorisers, who talked of nothing but the rights of man, and deliberately set as wide
a gulf as ruin and bloodshed could make between themselves and every incident or institution in the history of
their land. The statesman who had once declared, and
habitually proved, his preference for peace over even
truth, who had all his life surrounded himself with a
mental paradise of order and equilibrium, in a moment
found himself confronted by the stupendous and awful
spectre which a century of disorder had raised in its
supreme hour. It could not have been difficult for
any one who had studied Burke's character and career, to
foretell all that now came to pass with him.

It was from an English, and not from a French point
of view, that Burke was first drawn to write upon the
Revolution. The 4th of November was the anniversary
of the landing of the Prince of Orange, and the first act
in the Revolution of 1688. The members of an association which called itself the Revolution Society, chiefly
composed of Dissenters, but not without a mixture of
Churchmen, including a few peers and a good many members of the House of Commons, met as usual to hear a
sermon in commemoration of the glorious day. Dr. Price
was the preacher, and both in the morning sermon, and
in the speeches which followed in the festivities of the
afternoon, the French were held up to the loudest admiration, as having carried the principles of our own Revolution to a loftier height, and having opened boundless
hopes to mankind. By these harmless proceedings
Burke's anger and scorn were aroused to a pitch which
must seem to us, as it seemed to not a few of his contemporaries, singularly out of all proportion to its cause.
Deeper things were doubtless in silent motion within him.

He set to work upon a denunciation of Price's doctrines, with a velocity that reminds us of Aristotle's comparison of anger to the over-hasty servant, who runs off with all speed before he has listened to half the message. This was the origin of the *Reflections.* The design grew as the writer went on. His imagination took fire ; his memory quickened a throng of impressive associations ; his excited vision revealed to him a band of vain, petulant upstarts persecuting the ministers of a sacred religion, insulting a virtuous and innocent sovereign, and covering with humiliation the august daughter of the Cæsars ; his mind teemed with the sage maxims of the philosophy of things established, and the precepts of the gospel of order. Every courier that crossed the Channel supplied new material to his contempt and his alarm. He condemned the whole method and course of the French reforms. His judgment was in suspense no more. He no longer distrusted ; he hated, despised, and began to dread.

Men soon began to whisper abroad that Burke thought ill of what was going on over the water. When it transpired that he was writing a pamphlet, the world of letters was stirred with the liveliest expectation. The name of the author, the importance of the subject, and the singularity of his opinions, so Mackintosh informs us, all inflamed the public curiosity. Soon after Parliament met for the session (1790), the army estimates were brought up. Fox criticised the increase of our forces, and incidentally hinted something in praise of the French army, which had shown that a man could be a soldier without ceasing to be a citizen. Some days afterwards the subject was revived, and Pitt, as well as Fox, avowed himself hopeful of the good effect of the Revolution upon the order and government of France. Burke followed in a very

different vein, openly proclaiming that dislike and fear of
the Revolution which was to be the one ceaseless refrain of
all that he spoke or wrote for the rest of his life. He
deplored Fox's praise of the army for breaking their lawful
allegiance, and then he proceeded with ominous words to
the effect that, if any friend of his should concur in any
measures which should tend to introduce such a democracy
as that of France, he would abandon his best friends and
join with his worst enemies to oppose either the means or
the end. This has unanimously been pronounced one of
the most brilliant and effective speeches that Burke ever
made. Fox rose with distress on every feature, and
made the often-quoted declaration of his debt to Burke :—
" If all the political information I have learned from
books, all which I have gained from science, and all which
my knowledge of the world and its affairs has taught me,
were put into one scale, and the improvement which I
have derived from my right honourable friend's instruction
and conversation were placed in the other, I should be at
a loss to decide to which to give the preference. I have
learnt more from my right honourable friend, than from
all the men with whom I ever conversed." All seemed
likely to end in a spirit of conciliation, until Sheridan
rose, and in the plainest terms that he could find, expressed
his dissent from everything that Burke had said. Burke
immediately renounced his friendship. For the first
time in his life he found the sympathy of the House
vehemently on his side.

In the following month (March, 1790) this unpromising
incident was succeeded by an aberration which no rational man will now undertake to defend. Fox brought
forward a motion for the repeal of the Test and Corporation Acts. He did this in accordance with a recent sug-

gestion of Burke's own, that he should strengthen his political position by winning the support of the Dissenters. Burke himself had always denounced the Test Act as bad, and as an abuse of sacred things. To the amazement of everybody, and to the infinite scandal of his party, he now pronounced the Dissenters to be disaffected citizens, and refused to relieve them. Well might Fox say that Burke's words had filled him with grief and shame.

Meanwhile the great rhetorical fabric gradually arose. Burke revised, erased, moderated, strengthened, emphasized, wrote and re-wrote with indefatigable industry. With the manuscript constantly under his eyes, he lingered busily, pen in hand, over paragraphs and phrases, antitheses and apophthegms. The *Reflections* was no superb improvisation. Its composition recalls Palma Giovine's account of the mighty Titian's way of working ; how the master made his preparations with resolute strokes of a heavily-laden brush, and then turned his picture to the wall, and by-and-by resumed again, and then again and again, redressing, adjusting, modelling the light with a rub of his finger, or dabbing a spot of dark colour into some corner with a touch of his thumb, and finally working all his smirches, contrasts, abruptnesses, into the glorious harmony that we know. Burke was so unwearied in this insatiable correction and alteration, that the printer found it necessary, instead of making the changes marked upon the proof sheets, to set up the whole in type afresh. The work was upon the easel for exactly a year. It was November (1790) before the result came into the hands of the public. It was a small octavo of three hundred and fifty-six pages, in contents rather less than twice the present volume, bound in an unlettered wrapper of grey paper, and sold for five shillings. In less than twelve months it reached its eleventh edition, and it has been computed that not many short of thirty thousand copies were sold within the next six years.

The first curiosity had languished in the course of the long delay, but it was revived in its strongest force when the book itself appeared. A remarkable effect instantly followed. Before the *Reflections* was published, the predominant sentiment in England had been one of mixed astonishment and sympathy. Pitt had expressed this common mood both in the House of Commons and in private. It was impossible for England not to be amazed at the uprising of a nation whom they had been accustomed to think of as willing slaves, and it was impossible for her, when the scene did not happen to be the American colonies or Ireland, not to profess good wishes for the cause of emancipation all over the world. Apart from the natural admiration of a free people for a neighbour struggling to be free, England saw no reason to lament a blow to a sovereign and a government who had interfered on the side of her insurgent colonies. To this easy state of mind Burke's book put an immediate end. At once, as contemporaries assure us, it divided the nation into two parties. On both sides it precipitated opinion. With a long-resounding blast on his golden trumpet Burke had unfurled a new flag, and half the nation hurried to rally to it—that half which had scouted his views on America, which had bitterly disliked his plan of Economic Reform, which had mocked his ideas on religious toleration, and which a moment before had hated and reviled him beyond all men living, for his fierce tenacity in the impeachment of Warren Hastings. The King said to everybody who came near him that the book was a good book, a very good book, and every gentleman ought to read it. The

universities began to think of offering the scarlet gown of
their most honourable degree to the assailant of Price and
the Dissenters.   The great army of the indolent good, the
people who lead excellent lives and never use their reason,
took violent alarm.   The timorous, the weak-minded, the
bigoted, were suddenly awakened to a sense of what they
owed to themselves.   Burke gave them the key which
enabled them to interpret the Revolution in harmony with
their usual ideas and their temperament.

Reaction quickly rose to a high pitch.   One preacher in a
parish church in the neighbourhood of London celebrated
the anniversary of the Restoration of King Charles II. by a
sermon, in which the pains of eternal damnation were con-
fidently promised to political disaffection.   Romilly, men-
tioning to a friend that the *Reflections* had got into a fourteenth edition, wondered whether Burke was not rather
ashamed of his success.   It is when we come to the rank and
file of reaction, that we find it hard to forgive the man of
genius who made himself the organ of their selfishness, their
timidity, and their blindness.   We know, alas, that the
parts of his writings on French affairs to which they would
fly, were not likely to be the parts which calm men
now read with sympathy, but the scoldings, the scream-
ings, the unworthy vituperation with which, especially in
the latest of them, he attacked everybody who took part
in the Revolution, from Condorcet and Lafayette down to
Marat and Couthon.   It was the feet of clay that they
adored in their image, and not the head of fine gold and
the breasts and the arms of silver.

On the continent of Europe the excitement was as great
among the ruling classes as it was at home.   Mirabeau,
who had made Burke's acquaintance some years before in
England, and even been his guest at Beaconsfield, now

made the *Reflections* the text of more than one tremendous
philippic. Louis XVI. is said to have translated the book
into French with his own hand. Catherine of Russia,
Voltaire's adored Semiramis of the North, the benefactress
of Diderot, the ready helper of the philosophic party,
pressed her congratulations on the great pontiff of the old
order, who now thundered anathema against the philosophers and all their works.

It is important to remember the stage which the
Revolution had reached, when Burke was composing his
attack upon it. The year 1790 was precisely the
time when the hopes of the best men in France shone
most brightly, and seemed most reasonable. There had
been disorders, and Paris still had ferocity in her mien.
But Robespierre was an obscure figure on the back
benches of the Assembly. Nobody had ever heard of
Danton. The name of Republic had never been so much
as whispered. The King still believed that constitutional
monarchy would leave him as much power as he desired.
He had voluntarily gone to the National Assembly, and
in simple language had exhorted them all to imitate his
example by professing the single opinion, the single
interest, the single wish—attachment to the new constitution, and ardent desire for the peace and happiness of
France. The clergy, it is true, were violently irritated by
the spoliation of their goods, and the nobles had crossed
the Rhine, to brood impotently in the safety of Coblenz
over projects of a bloody revenge upon their country.
But France, meanwhile, paid little heed either to the
anger of the clergy or the menaces of the emigrant
nobles, and at the very moment when Burke was writing
his most sombre pages, Paris and the provinces were cele-
brating with transports of joy and enthusiasm the civic

oath, the federation, the restoration of concord to the land, the final establishment of freedom and justice in a regenerated France. This was the happy scene over which Burke suddenly stretched out the right arm of an inspired prophet, pointing to the cloud of thunder and darkness that was gathering on the hills, and proclaiming to them the doom that had been written upon the wall by the fingers of an inexorable hand. It is no wonder that when the cloud burst and the doom was fulfilled, men turned to Burke, as they went of old to Ahithophel, whose counsel was as if a man had inquired of the oracle of God.

It is not to our purpose to discuss all the propositions advanced in the *Reflections*, much less to reply to them. The book is like some temple, by whose structure and design we allow ourselves to be impressed, without being careful to measure the precise truth or fitness of the worship to which it was consecrated by its first founders. Just as the student of the *Politics* of Aristotle may well accept all the wisdom of it, without caring to protest at every turn against slavery as the basis of a society, so we may well cherish all the wisdom of the *Reflections*, at this distance of time, without marking as a rubric on every page that half of these impressive formulæ and inspiring declamations were irrelevant to the occasion which called them forth, and exercised for the hour an influence that was purely mischievous. Time permits to us this profitable lenity. In reading this, the first of his invectives, it is important for the sake of clearness of judgment to put from our minds the practical policy which Burke afterwards so untiringly urged upon his countrymen. As yet there is no exhortation to England to interfere, and we still listen to the voice of the states-

man, and are not deafened by the passionate cries of the
preacher of a crusade. When Burke wrote the *Reflections*,
he was justified in criticising the Revolution as an extraordinary movement, but still a movement professing
to be conducted on the principles of rational and practi-
cable politics. They were the principles to which competent onlookers like Jefferson and Morris had expected
the Assembly to conform, but to which the Assembly
never conformed for an instant. It was on the principles
of rational politics that Fox and Sheridan admired it.
On these principles Burke condemned it. He declared
that the methods of the Constituent Assembly, up to the
summer of 1790, were unjust, precipitate, destructive, and
without stability. Men had chosen to build their house
on the sands, and the winds and the seas would speedily
beat against it and overthrow it.

His prophecy was fulfilled to the letter. What is
still more important for the credit of his foresight is, that
not only did his prophecy come true, but it came true for
the reasons that he had fixed upon. It was, for instance,
the constitution of the Church, in which Burke saw the
worst of the many bad mistakes of the Assembly. History,
now slowly shaking herself free from the passions of a
century, agrees that the civil constitution of the clergy
was the measure which, more than any other, decisively
put an end to whatever hopes there might have been of
a peaceful transition from the old order to the new. A
still more striking piece of foresight is the prediction
of the despotism of the Napoleonic Empire. Burke
had compared the levelling policy of the Assembly in
their geometrical division of the departments, and their
isolation from one another of the bodies of the state, to the
treatment which a conquered country receives at the hands

of its conquerors. Like Romans in Greece or Macedon, the French innovators had destroyed the bonds of union, under colour of providing for the independence of each of their cities. " If the present project of a Republic should fail," Burke said, with a prescience really profound, "all securities to a moderate freedom fail with it. All the indirect restraints which mitigate despotism are removed; insomuch that, if monarchy should ever again obtain an entire ascendancy in France under this or any other dynasty, it will probably be, if not voluntarily tempered at setting out by the wise and virtuous counsels of the prince, the most completely arbitrary power that ever appeared on earth." Almost at the same moment Mirabeau was secretly writing to the King, that their plan of reducing all citizens to a single class would have delighted Richelieu. This equal surface, he said, facilitates the exercise of power, and many reigns in an absolute government would not have done as much as this single year of revolution, for the royal authority. Time showed that Burke and Mirabeau were right.

History ratifies nearly all Burke's strictures on the levity and precipitancy of the first set of actors in the revolutionary drama. No part of the *Reflections* is more energetic than the denunciation of geometric and literary methods ; and these are just what the modern explorer hits upon, as one of the fatal secrets of the catastrophe. De Tocqueville's chapter on the causes which made literary men the principal persons in France, and the effect which this had upon the Revolution (Bk. III. ch. i.), is only a little too cold to be able to pass for Burke's own. Quinet's work on the Revolution is one long sermon, full of eloquence and cogency, upon the incapacity and blindness of the men who undertook the conduct of a tremendous

crisis upon mere literary methods, without the moral
courage to obey the logic of their beliefs, with the student's
ignorance of the eager passion and rapid imagination of
multitudes of men, with the pedant's misappreciation of a
people, of whom it has been said by one of themselves,
that there never was a nation more led by its sensations,
and less by its principles.   Comte, again, points impressively to the Revolution as the period which illustrates
more decisively than another, the peril of confounding the
two great functions of speculation and political action :
and he speaks with just reprobation of the preposterous
idea in the philosophic politicians of the epoch, that
society was at their disposal, independent of its past
development, devoid of inherent impulses, and easily
capable of being morally regenerated by the mere modification of legislative rules.

   What then was it that, in the midst of so much per-
spicacity as to detail, blinded Burke at the time when he
wrote the *Reflections*, to the true nature of the movement ?
Is it not this, that he judges the Revolution as the solution
of a merely political question ?   If the Revolution had
been merely political, his judgment would have been
adequate.   The question was much deeper.   It was a
social question that burned under the surface of what
seemed no more than a modification of external arrangements.   That Burke was alive to the existence of social
problems, and that he was even tormented by them, we
know from an incidental passage in the *Reflections*. There
he tells us how often he had reflected, and never reflected
without feeling, upon the innumerable servile and degrading
occupations to which, by the social economy, so many
wretches are inevitably doomed.   He had pondered
whether there could be any means of rescuing these

unhappy people from their miserable industry, without
disturbing the natural course of things, and impeding the
great wheel of circulation which is turned by their labour.
This is the vein of that striking passage in his first composition, which I have already quoted (p. 16). Burke
did not yet see, and probably never saw, that one key to
the events which astonished and exasperated him, was
simply that the persons most urgently concerned had
taken the riddle which perplexed him, into their own
hands, and had in fiery earnest set about their own
deliverance. The pith of the Revolution, up to 1790,
was less the political constitution, of which Burke says so
much and so much that is true, but the social and economic transformation, of which he says so little. It was not
a question of the power of the King, or the measure of an
electoral circumscription, that made the Revolution ; it was
the iniquitous distribution of the taxes, the scourge of
the militia service, the scourge of the road service, the
destructive tyranny exercised in the vast preserves of
wild game, the vexatious rights and imposts of the lords
of manors, and all the other odious burdens and heavy
impediments on the prosperity of the thrifty and industrious part of the nation. If he had seen ever so clearly
that one of the most important sides of the Revolution
in progress was the rescue of the tiller of the soil, Burke
would still doubtless have viewed events with bitter suspicion. For the process could not be executed without
disturbing the natural course of things, and without
violating his principle that all changes should find us
with our minds tenacious of justice and tender of property. A closer examination than he chose to give, of
the current administration alike of justice and of property
under the old system, would have explained to him that

an hour had come in which the spirit of property and of
justice compelled a supersession of the letter.

If Burke had insisted on rigidly keeping sensibility to
the wrongs of the French people out of the discussion, on
the ground that the whole subject was one for positive
knowledge and logical inference, his position would have
been intelligible and defensible. He followed no such
course. His pleading turns constantly to arguments
from feeling ; but it is always to feeling on one side, and
to a sensibility that is only alive to the consecrated force
of historic associations. How much pure and uncontrolled
emotion had to do with what ought to have been the
reasoned judgments of his understanding, we know on his
own evidence. He had sent the proof-sheets of a part of
his book to Sir Philip Francis. They contained the
famous passage describing the French Queen as he had
seen her seventeen years before at Versailles. Francis
bluntly wrote to him that, in his opinion, all Burke's
eloquence about Marie Antoinette was no better than pure
foppery, and he referred to the Queen herself as no better
than Messalina. Burke was so excited by this, that his
son, in a rather officious letter, begged Francis not to
repeat such stimulating remonstrance. What is interesting in the incident, is Burke's own reply. He knew
nothing, he said, of the story of Messalina, and declined
the obligation of proving judicially the virtues of all those
whom he saw suffering wrong and contumely, before he
endeavoured to interest others in their sufferings, and
before endeavouring to kindle horror against midnight
assassins at backstairs and their more wicked abettors in
pulpits. And then he went on, " I tell you again
that the recollection of the manner in which I saw the
Queen of France in the year 1774 [1773], and the con-

trast between that brilliancy, splendour, and beauty, with
the prostrate homage of a nation to her, and the abomin-
able scene of 1789 which I was describing, *did* draw
tears from me and wetted my paper. These tears came
again into my eyes almost as often as I looked at the
description—they may again."

The answer was obvious. It was well to pity the un-
merited agonies of Marie Antoinette, though as yet, we
must remember, she had suffered nothing beyond the in-
dignities of the days of October at Versailles. But did
not the protracted agonies of a nation deserve the tribute
of a tear? As Paine asked, were men to weep over the
plumage, and forget the dying bird? The bulk of the
people must labour, Burke told them, " to obtain what by
labour can be obtained ; and when they find, as they
commonly do, the success disproportioned to the endeavour, they must be taught their consolation in the final
proportions of eternal justice." When we know that a
Lyons silk weaver, working as hard as he could for over
seventeen hours a day, could not earn money enough to
procure the most bare and urgent necessaries of subsist-
ence, we may know with what benignity of brow eternal
justice must have presented herself in the garret of
that hapless wretch. It was no idle abstraction, no metaphysical right of man for which the French cried, but
only the practical right of being permitted, by their own
toil, to save themselves and the little ones about their
knees from hunger and cruel death. The *mainmortable*
serfs of ecclesiastics are variously said to have been a
million and a million and a half at the time of the Revolution. Burke's horror, as he thought of the priests and
prelates who left palaces and dignities to earn a scanty
living by the drudgery of teaching their language in

M

strange lands, should have been alleviated by the thought
that a million or more of men were rescued from ghastly
material misery. Are we to be so overwhelmed with sor-
row over the pitiful destiny of the men of exalted rank and
sacred function, as to have no tears for the forty thousand
serfs in the gorges of the Jura, who were held in dead-
hand by the Bishop of Saint-Claude?

The simple truth is that Burke did not know enough
of the subject about which he was writing. When he
said, for instance, that the French before 1789 possessed
all the elements of a constitution that might be made
nearly as good as could be wished, he said what many of
his contemporaries knew, and what all subsequent investigation and meditation have proved, to be recklessly ill-con-
sidered and untrue. As to the social state of France, his
information was still worse. He saw the dangers and disorders of the new system, but he saw a very little way
indeed into the more cruel dangers and disorders of the old.
Mackintosh replied to the *Reflections* with manliness and
temperance in the *Vindiciæ Gallicæ.* Thomas Paine
replied to them with an energy, courage, and eloquence
worthy of his cause, in the *Rights of Man.* But the
substantial and decisive reply to Burke came from his
former correspondent, the farmer at Bradfield in Suffolk.
Arthur Young published his *Travels in France* some
eighteen months after the *Reflections* (1792), and the
pages of the twenty-first chapter, in which he closes his
performance, as a luminous criticism of the most important side of the Revolution, are worth a hundred times
more than Burke, Mackintosh, and Paine all put together.
Young afterwards became panic-stricken, but his book remained. There the writer plainly enumerates without
trope or invective the intolerable burdens under which

the great mass of the French people had for long years been groaning. It was the removal of these burdens that made the very heart's core of the Revolution, and gave to France that new life which so soon astonished and terrified Europe. Yet Burke seems profoundly unconscious of the whole of them. He even boldly asserts that, when the several orders met in their bailliages in 1789, to choose their representatives and draw up their grievances and instructions, in no one of these instructions did they charge, or even hint at, any of those things which had drawn upon the usurping Assembly the detestation of the rational part of mankind. He could not have made a more enormous blunder. There was not a single great change made by the Assembly, which had not been demanded in the lists of grievances that had been sent up by the nation to Versailles. The division of the kingdom into districts, and the proportioning of the representation to taxes and population; the suppression of the intendants ; the suppression of all monks and the sale of their goods and estates ; the abolition of feudal rights, duties and services ; the alienation of the King's domains ; the demolition of the Bastille ; these and all else were in the prayers of half the petitions that the country had laid at the feet of the King.

If this were merely an incidental blunder in a fact, it might be of no importance. But it was a blunder which went to the very root of the discussion. The fact that France was now at the back of the Assembly, inspiring its counsels and ratifying its decrees, was the cardinal element, and that is the fact which at this stage Burke systematically ignored. That he should have so ignored it, left him in a curious position, for it left him without any rational explanation of the sources of the policy which

M 2

kindled his indignation and contempt. A publicist can
never be sure of his position, until he can explain to himself even what he does not wish to justify to others.
Burke thought it enough to dwell upon the immense
number of lawyers in the Assembly, and to show that
lawyers are naturally bad statesmen. He did not look
the state of things steadily in the face. It was no easy
thing to do, but Burke was a man who ought to
have done it. He set all down to the ignorance, folly,
and wickedness of the French leaders. This was as
shallow as the way in which his enemies, the philosophers, used to set down the superstition of eighteen
centuries to the craft of priests, and all defects in the
government of Europe to the cruelty of tyrants. How it
came about that priests and tyrants acquired their irresistible power over men's minds, they never inquired. And
Burke never inquired into the enthusiastic acquiescence
of the nation, and, what was most remarkable of all,
the acquiescence of the army, in the strong measures
of the Assembly. Burke was in truth so appalled
by the magnitude of the enterprise on which France
had embarked, that he utterly forgot for once the necessity
in political affairs, of seriously understanding the origi-
nating conditions of things. He was strangely content
with the explanations that came from the malignants
at Coblenz, and he actually told Francis that he charged
the disorders not on the mob, but on the Duke of
of Orleans and Mirabeau, on Barnave and Bailly, on
Lameth and Lafayette, who had spent immense sums
of money, and used innumerable arts, to stir up the
populace throughout France to the commission of the
enormities that were shocking the conscience of Europe.
His imagination broke loose. His practical reason was

VIII.]   BURKE'S POLITICAL MYSTICISM.   165

mastered by something that was deeper in him than reason.

This brings me to remark a really singular trait. In spite of the predominance of practical sagacity, of the habits and spirit of public business, of vigorous actuality in Burke's character, yet at the bottom of all his thoughts about communities and governments there lay a certain mysticism. It was no irony, no literary trope, when he talked of our having taught the American husbandman "piously to believe in the mysterious virtue of wax and parchment." He was using no otiose epithet, when he described the disposition of a stupendous wisdom, "moulding together the great mysterious incorporation of the human race." To him there actually was an element of mystery in the cohesion of men in societies, in political obedience, in the sanctity of contract; in all that fabric of law and charter and obligation, whether written or unwritten, which is the sheltering bulwark between civilization and barbarism. When reason and history had contributed all that they could to the explanation, it seemed to him as if the vital force, the secret of organization, the binding framework, must still come from the impenetrable regions beyond reasoning and beyond history. There was another great conservative writer of that age, whose genius was aroused into a protest against the revolutionary spirit, as vehement as Burke's. This was Joseph de Maistre, one of the most learned, witty, and acute of all reactionary philosophers. De Maistre wrote a book on the Generative Principle of Political Constitutions. He could only find this principle in the operation of occult and supernatural forces, producing the half-divine legislators who figure mysteriously in the early history of nations. Hence he held, and with astonishing ingenuity enforced, the doctrine that nothing

else could deliver Europe from the Satanic forces of revolution—he used the word Satanic in all literal seriousness
—save the divinely inspired supremacy of the Pope.   No
natural operations seemed at all adequate either to produce or to maintain the marvel of a coherent society.
We are reminded of a professor who, in the fantastic
days of geology, explained the Pyramids of Egypt to
be the remains of a volcanic eruption, which had forced
its way upwards by a slow and stately motion ; the
hieroglyphs were crystalline formations ; and the shaft of
the great Pyramid was the air-hole of a volcano.   De
Maistre preferred a similar explanation of the monstrous
structures of modern society.   The hand of man could
never have reared, and could never uphold them.   If we
cannot say that Burke laboured in constant travail with
the same perplexity, it is at least true that he was keenly
alive to it, and that one of the reasons why he dreaded to
see a finger laid upon a single stone of a single political
edifice, was his consciousness that he saw no answer to
the perpetual enigma how any of these edifices had ever
been built, and how the passion, violence, and waywardness of the natural man had ever been persuaded to bow
their necks to the strong yoke of a common social discipline.   Never was mysticism more unseasonable ; never
was an hour when men needed more carefully to remember
Burke's own wise practical precept, when he was talking
about the British rule in India, that we must throw a
sacred veil over the beginnings of government.   Many
woes might perhaps have been saved to Europe, if
Burke had applied this maxim to the government of the
new France.

Much has always been said about the inconsistency between Burke's enmity to the Revolution, and his enmity to

Lord North in one set of circumstances, and to Warren
Hastings in another. The pamphleteers of the day made
selections from the speeches and tracts of his happier time,
and the seeming contrast had its effect. More candid opponents admitted then, as all competent persons admit now,
that the inconsistency was merely verbal and superficial.
Watson, the Bishop of Llandaff, was only one of many
who observed very early that this was the unmistakable
temper of Burke's mind. " I admired, as everybody did,"
he said, " the talents, but not the principles of Mr. Burke ;
his opposition to the Clerical Petition [for relaxation of
subscription, 1772], first excited my suspicion of his being
a High Churchman in religion, and a Tory, perhaps an
aristocratic Tory, in the state." Burke had indeed never
been anything else than a conservative. He was like
Falkland, who had bitterly assailed Strafford and Finch
on the same principles on which, after the outbreak of the
civil war, he consented to be secretary of state to King
Charles. Coleridge is borne out by a hundred passages,
when he says that in Burke's writings at the beginning of
the American Revolution and in those at the beginning of
the French Revolution, the principles are the same and
the deductions are the same ; the practical inferences are
almost opposite in the one case from those drawn in the
other, yet in both equally legitimate. It would be better
to say that they would have been equally legitimate, if
Burke had been as right in his facts, and as ample in his
knowledge in the case of France, as he was in the case of
America. We feel, indeed, that partly from want of this
knowledge, he has gone too far from some of the wise
maxims of an earlier time. What has become of the
doctrine that all great public collections of men—he
was then speaking of the House of Commons—" possess

a marked love of virtue and an abhorrence of vice."[1] Why was the French Assembly not to have the benefit of this admirable generalisation? What has become of all those sayings about the presumption, in all disputes between nations and rulers, " being at least upon a par in favour of the people;" and a populace never rebelling from passion for attack, but from impatience of suffering? And where is now that strong dictum, in the letter to the Sheriffs of Bristol, that " general rebellions and revolts of a whole people never were *encouraged*, now or at any time; they are always *provoked*"?

When all these things have been noted, to hold a man to his formulæ without reference to their special application, is pure pedantry. Burke was the last man to lay down any political proposition not subject to the ever varying interpretation of circumstances, and independently of the particular use which was to be made of it. Nothing universal, he had always said, can be rationally affirmed on any moral or political subject. The lines of morality, again, are never ideal lines of mathematics, but are broad and deep as well as long, admitting of exceptions, and demanding modifications. " These exceptions and modifications are made, not by the process of logic, but by the rules of prudence. Prudence is not only first in rank of the virtues, political and moral, but she is the director, the regulator, the standard of them all. As no moral questions are ever abstract questions, this, before I judge upon any abstract proposition, must be embodied in circumstances; for, since things are right and wrong, morally speaking, only by their relation and connection with other things, this very question of what it is politi-

[1] *American Taxation.*

cally right to grant, depends upon its relation to its effects." "Circumstances," he says, never weary of laying down his great notion of political method, "give, in reality, to every political principle its distinguishing colour and discriminating effect. The circumstances are what render every civil and political scheme beneficial or obnoxious to mankind."

This is at once the weapon with which he would have defended his own consistency, and attacked the absolute proceedings in France. He changed his front, but he never changed his ground. He was not more passionate against the proscription in France, than he had been against the suspension of Habeas Corpus in the American war. "I flatter myself," he said in the *Reflections*, "that I love a manly, moral, regulated liberty." Ten years before he had said, "The liberty, the only liberty I mean, is a liberty connected with order." The court tried to regulate liberty too severely. It found in him an inflexible opponent. Demagogues tried to remove the regulations of liberty. They encountered in him the bitterest and most unceasing of all remonstrants. The arbitrary majority in the House of Commons forgot for whose benefit they held power, from whom they derived their authority, and in what description of government it was that they had a place. Burke was the most valiant and strenuous champion in the ranks of the independent minority. He withstood to the face the King and the King's friends. He withstood to the face Charles Fox and the Friends of the People. He may have been wrong in both, or in either, but it is unreasonable to tell us that he turned back in his course; that he was a revolutionist in 1770, and a reactionist in 1790; that he was in his sane mind when he opposed the supremacy of the Court, but

that his reason was tottering when he opposed the
supremacy of the Faubourg Saint Antoine.

There is no part of Burke's career at which we may not
find evidence of his instinctive and undying repugnance
to the critical or revolutionary spirit and all its works.
From the early days when he had parodied Bolingbroke,
down to the later time when he denounced Condorcet as
a fanatical atheist, with "every disposition to the lowest
as well as the highest and most determined villanies," he
invariably suspected or denounced everybody, virtuous
or vicious, high-minded or ignoble, who inquired with
too keen a scrutiny into the foundations of morals, of
religion, of social order.   To examine with a curious or
unfavourable eye the bases of established opinions, was to
show a leaning to anarchy, to atheism, or to unbridled
libertinism.   Already we have seen how, three years after
the publication of his *Thoughts on the Present Discontents*,
and seventeen years before the composition of the *Reflections*, he denounced the philosophers with a fervour and
a vehemence which he never afterwards surpassed.   When
some of the clergy petitioned to be relieved from some of
the severities of subscription, he had resisted them on
the bold ground that the truth of a proposition deserves
less attention, than the effect of adherence to it upon the
established order of things.   " I will not enter into the
question," he told the House of Commons, "how much
truth is preferable to peace.   Perhaps truth may be far
better.   But as we have scarcely ever the same certainty
in the one that we have in the other, I would, unless the
truth were evident indeed, hold fast to peace."   In that
intellectual restlessness, to which the world is so deeply
indebted, Burke could recognize but scanty merit.   Himself the most industrious and active-minded of men, he

was ever sober in cutting the channels of his activity, and he would have had others equally moderate. Perceiving that plain and righteous conduct is the end of life in this world, he prayed men not to be over curious in searching for, and handling, and again handling, the theoretic base on which the prerogatives of virtue repose. Provided that there was peace, that is to say, so much of fair happiness and content as is compatible with the conditions of the human lot, Burke felt that a too great inquisitiveness as to its foundations was not only idle but cruel.

If the world continues to read the *Reflections*, and reads it with a new admiration that is not diminished by the fact that on the special issue its tendency is every day more clearly discerned to have been misleading, we may be sure that it is not for the sake of such things as the precise character of the Revolution of 1688, where, for that matter, constitutional writers have shown abundantly that Burke was nearly as much in the wrong as Dr. Sacheverell. Nor has the book lived merely by its gorgeous rhetoric and high emotions, though these have been contributing elements. It lives because it contains a sentiment, a method, a set of informal principles, which, awakened into new life after the Revolution, rapidly transformed the current ways of thinking and feeling about all the most serious objects of our attention, and have powerfully helped to give a richer substance to all modern literature. In the *Reflections* we have the first great sign that the ideas on government and philosophy which Locke had been the chief agent in setting into European circulation, and which had carried all triumphantly before them throughout the century, did not comprehend the whole truth nor the deepest truth about human character—the

relations of men and the union of men in society. It has
often been said that the armoury from which the French
philosophers of the eighteenth century borrowed their
weapons, was furnished from England, and it may be added
as truly that the reaction against that whole scheme of
thought came from England. In one sense we may call the
Reflections a political pamphlet, but it is much more than
this, just as the movement against which it was levelled
was much more than a political movement. The Revolution rested on a philosophy, and Burke confronted it with
an antagonistic philosophy. Those are but superficial
readers who fail to see at how many points Burke, while
seeming only to deal with the French monarchy and the
British constitution, with Dr. Price and Marie Antoinette,
was in fact, and exactly because he dealt with them in the
comprehensive spirit of true philosophy, turning men's
minds to an attitude from which not only the political
incidents of the hour, but the current ideas about religion,
psychology, the very nature of human knowledge, would
all be seen in a changed light and clothed in new colour.
All really profound speculation about society comes in
time to touch the heart of every other object of speculation, not by directly contributing new truths or directly
corroborating old ones, but by setting men to consider the
consequences to life of different opinions on these abstract
subjects, and their relations to the great paramount interests of society, however those interests may happen at
the time to be conceived. Burke's book marks a turning
point in literary history, because it was the signal for
that reaction over the whole field of thought, into which
the Revolution drove many of the finest minds of the
next generation, by showing the supposed consequences of
pure individualistic rationalism.

We need not attempt to work out the details of this ex-
tension of a political reaction into a universal reaction in
philosophy and poetry. Any one may easily think out
for himself what consequences in act and thought, as well
as in government, would be likely to flow, for example,
from one of the most permanently admirable sides of
Burke's teaching—his respect for the collective reason
of men, and his sense of the impossibility in politics
and morals of considering the individual apart from
the experience of the race. " We are afraid," he says,
" to put men to live and trade each on his own private
stock of reason, because we suspect that this stock in each
man is small, and that the individuals would do better to
avail themselves of the general bank and capital of nations
and of ages. *Many of our men of speculation, instead of
exploding general prejudices, employ their sagacity to discover the latent wisdom which prevails in them.* If they
find what they seek, and they seldom fail, they think it
more wise to continue the prejudice with the reason involved, than to cast away the coat of prejudice, and to
leave nothing but the naked reason : because prejudice
with its reason has a motive to give action to that reason,
and an affection which will give it permanence. Prejudice
is of ready application in the emergency ; it previously
engages the mind in a steady course of wisdom and virtue,
and does not leave the man hesitating in the moment of
decision, sceptical, puzzled, and unresolved. Prejudice
renders a man's virtue his habit, and not a series of unconnected acts. Through just prejudice, his duty becomes
a part of his nature." Is not this to say, in other words,
that in every man the substantial foundations of action
consist of the accumulated layers which various generations
of ancestors have placed for him ; that the greater part of

our sentiments act most effectively when they act most
mechanically, and by the methods of an unquestioned
system; that although no rule of conduct or spring of
action ought to endure, which does not repose in sound
reason, yet this naked reason is in itself a less effective
means of influencing action, than when it exists as one
part of a fabric of ancient and endeared association?
Interpreted by a mobile genius, and expanded by a poetic
imagination, all this became the foundation from which
the philosophy of Coleridge started, and, as Mill has
shown in a famous essay, Coleridge was the great apostle
of the conservative spirit in England in its best form.

Though Burke here, no doubt, found a true base for the
philosophy of order, yet perhaps Condorcet or Barnave
might have justly asked him whether, when we thus realize
the strong and immovable foundations which are laid in our
character before we are born, there could be any occasion,
as a matter of fact, for that vehement alarm which moved
Burke lest a few lawyers, by a score of parchment decrees,
should overthrow the venerated sentiments of Europe about
justice and about property? Should he not have known
better than most men the force of the self-protecting
elements of society?

This is not a convenient place for discussing the issues
between the school of order and the school of progress.
It is enough to have marked Burke's position in one of
them. The *Reflections* places him among the great Conser-
vatives of history. Perhaps the only Englishman with
whom in this respect he may be compared, is Sir Thomas
More, that virtuous and eloquent reactionist of the sixteenth century. More abounded in light, in intellectual
interests, in single-minded care for the common weal. He
was as anxious as any man of his time for the improved

ordering of the Church, but he could not endure that reformation should be bought at the price of breaking up the ancient spiritual unity of Europe. He was willing to slay and be slain rather than he would tolerate the destruction of the old faith, or assent to the violence of the new statecraft. He viewed Thomas Cromwell's policy of reformation, just as Burke viewed Mirabeau's policy of revolution. Burke too, we may be very sure, would as willingly have sent Mirabeau and Bailly to prison or the block as More sent Phillips to the Tower and Bainham to the stake. For neither More nor Burke was of the gentle contemplative spirit, which the first disorder of a new society just bursting into life merely overshadows with saddening regrets and poetic gloom. The old harmony was to them so bound up with the purpose and meaning of life, that to wage active battle for the gods of their reverence was the irresistible instinct of self-preservation. More had an excuse which Burke had not, for the principle of persecution was accepted by the best minds of the sixteenth century, but by the best minds of the eighteenth it was emphatically repudiated.

Another illustrious name of Burke's own era rises to our lips, as we ponder mentally the too scanty list of those who have essayed the great and hardy task of reconciling order with progress. Turgot is even a more imposing figure than Burke himself. The impression made upon us by the pair is indeed very different, for Turgot was austere, reserved, distant, a man of many silences, and much suspense ; while Burke, as we know, was imaginative, exuberant, unrestrained, and, like some of the greatest actors on the stage of human affairs, he had associated his own personality with the prevalence of right ideas and good influences. In Turgot, on the other hand, we dis-

cern something of the isolation, the sternness, the disdain-
ful melancholy of Tacitus. He even rises out of the eager,
bustling, shrill-tongued crowd of the Voltairean age with
some of that austere moral indignation and haughty
astonishment, with which Dante had watched the stub-
born ways of men centuries before. On one side Turgot
shared the conservatism of Burke, though, perhaps, he
would hardly have given it that name. He habitually
corrected the headlong insistence of the revolutionary
philosophers, his friends, by reminding them that neither
pity, nor benevolence, nor hope can ever dispense with
justice ; and he could never endure to hear of great changes
being wrought at the cost of this sovereign quality. Like
Burke, he held fast to the doctrine that everything must
be done for the multitude, but nothing by them. Like
Burke, he realized how close are the links that bind the
successive generations of men, and make up the long chain
of human history. Like Burke, he never believed that
the human mind has any spontaneous inclination to welcome pure truth. Here, however, is visible between them a
hard line of division. It is not error, said Turgot, which
opposes the progress of truth ; it is indolence, obstinacy,
and the spirit of routine. But then Turgot enjoined upon
us to make it the aim of life to do battle in ourselves and
others with all this indolence, obstinacy, and spirit of
routine in the world ; while Burke, on the contrary, gave
to these bad things gentler names, he surrounded them
with the picturesque associations of the past, and in the
great world-crisis of his time he threw all his passion and
all his genius on their side. Will any reader doubt which
of these two types of the school of order and justice,
both of them noble, is the more valuable for the race, and
the worthier and more stimulating ideal for the individual ?

It is not certain that Burke was not sometimes for a moment startled by the suspicion that he might unawares be fighting against the truth. In the midst of flaming and bitter pages, we now and again feel a cool breath from the distant region of a half-pensive tolerance. " I do not think," he says at the close of the *Reflections*, to the person to whom they were addressed, " that my sentiments are likely to alter yours. I do not know that they ought. You are young ; you cannot guide, but must follow, the fortune of your country. But hereafter they may be of some use to you, in some future form which your commonwealth may take. In the present it can hardly remain ; but before its final settlement, it may be obliged to pass, as one of our poets says, ' through great varieties of untried being,' and in all its transmigrations to be purified by fire and blood."

He felt in the midst of his hate that what he took for seething chaos, might after all be the struggle upwards of the germs of order. Among the later words that he wrote on the Revolution were these :—" If a great change is to be made in human affairs, the minds of men will be fitted to it ; the general opinions and feelings will draw that way. Every fear, every hope will forward it ; and then they who persist in opposing this mighty current in human affairs, will appear rather to resist the decrees of Providence itself, than the mere designs of men." We can only regret that these rays of the *mens divinior* did not shine with a more steadfast light; and that a spirit which, amid the sharp press of manifold cares and distractions, had ever vibrated with lofty sympathies, was not now more constant to its faith in the beneficent powers and processes of the Unseen Time.

N

CHAPTER IX.

FOR some months after the publication of the *Reflections,*
Burke kept up the relations of an armed peace with his
old political friends.   The impeachment went on, and in
December (1790) there was a private meeting on the
business connected with it, between Pitt, Burke, Fox, and
Dundas, at the house of the Speaker.   It was described
by one who knew, as most snug and amiable, and there
seems to have been a general impression in the world at
this moment, that Fox might by some means be induced
to join Pitt.   What troubled the slumbers of good Whigs
like Gilbert Elliott, was the prospect of Fox committing
himself too strongly on French affairs.   Burke himself
was in the deepest dejection at the prospect ; for Fox
did not cease to express the most unqualified disapproval
of the *Reflections;* he thought that, even in point of composition, it was the worst thing that Burke had ever
published.   It was already feared that his friendship for
Sheridan was drawing him further away from Burke,
with whom Sheridan had quarrelled, into a course of
politics that would both damage his own reputation, and
break up the strong union of which the Duke of Portland
was the nominal head.

New floods in France had not yet carried back the
ship of state into raging waters. Pitt was thinking so
little of danger from that country, that he had plunged
into a policy of intervention in the affairs of eastern
Europe. When writers charge Burke with breaking
violently in upon Pitt's system of peace abroad and
reform at home, they overlook the fact that before Burke
had begun to preach his crusade against the Jacobins, Pitt
had already prepared a war with Russia. The nation
refused to follow. They agreed with Fox that it was no
concern of theirs whether or not Russia took from Turkey
the country between the Boug and Dniester; they felt
that British interests would be more damaged by the expenses of a war, than by the acquisition by Russia of
Ockzakow. Pitt was obliged to throw up the scheme,
and to extricate himself as well as he could from rash
engagements with Prussia. It was on account of his services to the cause of peace on this occasion, that Catherine
ordered the Russian ambassador to send her a bust of Fox
in white marble, to be placed in her colonnade between
Demosthenes and Cicero. We may take it for granted
that after the Revolution rose to its full height, the bust
of Fox accompanied that of Voltaire down to the cellar of
the Hermitage.

While the affair of the Russian armament was still
occupying the minister, an event of signal importance
happened in the ranks of his political adversaries. The
alliance which had lasted between Burke and Fox for
five and twenty years, came to a sudden end, and this
rift gradually widened into a destructive breach throughout the party. There is no parallel in our parliamentary
history to the fatal scene. In Ireland, indeed, only eight
years before, Flood and Grattan, after fighting side by

side for many years, had all at once sprung upon one
another in the Parliament House with the fury of vultures:
Flood had screamed to Grattan that he was a mendicant
patriot, and Grattan had called Flood an ill-omened bird
of night, with a sepulchral note, a cadaverous aspect,
and a broken beak. The Irish, like the French, have
the art of making things dramatic, and Burke was the
greatest of Irishmen. On the opening of the session
of 1791, the government had introduced a bill for the
better government of Canada. It introduced questions
about church establishments and hereditary legislators.
In discussing these, Fox made some references to France.
It was impossible to refer to France without touching the
Reflections on the French Revolution. Burke was not
present, but he heard what Fox had said, and before long
Fox again introduced French affairs in a debate on the
Russian armament. Burke rose in violent heat of mind
to reply, but the House would not hear him. He resolved
to speak when the time came for the Canada Bill to be
recommitted. Meanwhile some of his friends did all that
they could to dissuade him from pressing the matter
further. Even the Prince of Wales is said to have
written him a letter. There were many signs of the
rupture that was so soon to come in the Whig ranks.
Men so equally devoted to the common cause as Windham and Elliot nearly came to a quarrel at a dinner-
party at Lord Malmesbury's, on the subject of Burke's
design to speak ; and Windham, who for the present sided
with Fox, enters in his diary that he was glad to escape
from the room without speaking to the man whom, since
the death of Doctor Johnson, he revered before all
others.

On the day appointed for the Canada Bill, Fox called

at Burke's house, and after some talk on Burke's intention to speak, and on other matters, they walked down
to Westminster and entered the House together, as they
had so many a time done before but were never to do
again. They found that the debate had been adjourned,
and it was not until May 6th that Burke had an opportunity of explaining himself on the Revolution in France.
He had no sooner risen, than interruptions broke out from
his own side, and a scene of great disorder followed. Burke
was incensed beyond endurance by this treatment, for even
Fox and Windham had taken part in the tumult against
him.   With much bitterness he commented on Fox's previous eulogies of the Revolution, and finally there came
the fatal words of severance.   " It is indiscreet," he said,
"at any period, but especially at my time of life, to pro-
voke enemies, or give my friends occasion to desert me.
Yet if my firm and steady adherence to the British Constitution place me in such a dilemma, I am ready to risk
it, and with my last words to exclaim, ' Fly from the
French Constitution.' "   Fox at this point eagerly called
to him that there was no loss of friends.   " Yes, yes,"
cried Burke, "there is a loss of friends. I know the price
of my conduct.   I have done my duty at the price of my
friend.   Our friendship is at an end."
     The members who sat on the same side were aghast at
proceedings which went beyond their worst apprehensions.
Even the ministerialists were shocked.   Pitt agreed much
more with Fox than with Burke, but he would have been
more than human if he had not watched with complacency
his two most formidable adversaries turning their swords
against one another.   Wilberforce, who was more disinterested, lamented the spectacle as shameful.   In the galleries there was hardly a dry eye. Fox, as might have

been expected from his warm and generous nature,
was deeply moved, and is described as weeping even
to sobbing. He repeated his former acknowledgment
of his debt to Burke, and he repeated his former ex·
pression of faith in the blessings which the abolition of royal despotism would bring to France. With
unabated vehemence Burke again rose to denounce the
French Constitution,—"a building composed of untem-
pered mortar—the work of Goths and Vandals, where
everything was disjointed and inverted." After a short
rejoinder from Fox, the scene came to a close, and the
once friendly intercourse between the two heroes was at an
end. When they met in the Managers' box in Westminster
Hall on the business of Hastings's trial, they met with the
formalities of strangers. There is a story that when Burke
left the House on the night of the quarrel it was raining,
and Mr. Curwen, a member of the Opposition, took him
home in his carriage. Burke at once began to declaim
against the French. Curwen dropped some remark on the
other side. " What ! " Burke cried out, grasping the check-
string, " are you one of these people ! Set me down." It
needed all Curwen's force to keep him where he was ; and
when they reached his house, Burke stepped out without
saying a single word.

We may agree that all this did not indicate the perfect
sobriety and self-control proper to a statesman, in what was
a serious crisis both to his party and to Europe. It was about
this time that Burke said to Addington, who was then
Speaker of the House of Commons, that he was not well. " I
eat too much, Speaker," he said, "I drink too much, and I
sleep too little." It is even said that he felt the final breach
with Fox as a relief from unendurable suspense ; and he
quoted the lines about Æneas, after he had finally resolved

to quit Dido and the Carthaginian shore, at last being
able to snatch slumber in his ship's tall stern.   There can
be no doubt how severe had been the tension.   Yet the
performance to which Burke now applied himself, is one
of the gravest and most reasonable of all his compositions.   He felt it necessary to vindicate the fundamental
consistency between his present and his past.   We have
no difficulty in imagining the abuse to which he was exposed from those whose abuse gave him pain.   In a country governed by party, a politician who quits the allies of
a lifetime, must expect to pay the penalty.   The Whig
papers told him that he was expected to surrender his seat
in Parliament.   They imputed to him all sorts of sinister
motives.   His name was introduced into ironical toasts.
For a whole year there was scarcely a member of his
former party who did not stand aloof from him.   Windham, when the feeling was at its height, sent word to a
host that he would rather not meet Burke at dinner.   Dr.
Parr, though he thought Mr. Burke the greatest man upon
earth, declared himself most indignantly and most fixedly
on the side of Mr. Sheridan and Mr. Fox.   The Duke of
Portland, though always described as strongly and fondly
attached to him, and Gilbert Elliot, who thought that
Burke was right in his views on the Revolution, and right
in expressing them, still could not forgive the open catastrophe, and for many months all the old habits of intimacy
among them were entirely broken off.

Burke did not bend to the storm.   He went down to
Margate, and there finished the *Appeal from the New to
the Old Whigs*.   Meanwhile he dispatched his son to
Coblenz to give advice to the royalist exiles, who were
then mainly in the hands of Calonne, one of the very
worst of the ministers whom Louis XVI. had tried be-

tween his dismissal of Turgot in 1774, and the meeting of
the States-General in 1789. This measure was taken at
the request of Calonne, who had visited Burke at Margate.
The English government did not disapprove of it, though
they naturally declined to invest either young Burke or
any one else with authority from themselves. As little
came of the mission as might have been expected from
the frivolous, unmanly, and enraged spirit of those to
whom it was addressed.

In August (1791), while Richard Burke was at Coblenz,
the *Appeal* was published. This was the last piece that
Burke wrote on the Revolution, in which there is any
pretence of measure, sobriety, and calm judgment in face
of a formidable and perplexing crisis. Henceforth it is
not political philosophy, but the minatory exhortation of a
prophet. We deal no longer with principles and ideas,
but with a partisan denunciation of particular acts, and a
partisan incitement to a given practical policy. We may
appreciate the policy as we choose, but our appreciation of
Burke as a thinker and a contributor to political wisdom
is at an end. He is now only Demosthenes thundering
against Philip, or Cicero shrieking against Mark Antony.

The *Reflections* had not been published many months,
before Burke wrote the *Letter to a Member of the National
Assembly* (January, 1791), in which strong disapproval
had grown into furious hatred. It contains the elaborate
diatribe against Rousseau, the grave panegyric on Cromwell
for choosing Hale to be Chief Justice, and a sound criticism
on the laxity and want of foresight in the manner in which
the States-General had been convened. Here first Burke
advanced to the position that it might be the duty of
other nations to interfere to restore the King to his rightful
authority, just as England and Prussia had interfered to

save Holland from confusion, as they had interfered to preserve the hereditary constitution in the Austrian Nether-
lands, and as Prussia had interfered to snatch even the
malignant and the turban'd Turk from the pounce of
the Russian eagle.   Was not the King of France as
much an object of policy and compassion, as the Grand
Seignior ?   As this was the first piece in which Burke
hinted at a crusade, so it was the first in which he began
to heap upon the heads, not of Hébert, Fouquier-Tin-
ville, Billaud, nor even of Robespierre or Danton—for
none of these had yet been heard of—but of able and
conscientious men in the Constituent Assembly, language
of a virulence which Fox once said seriously that
Burke had picked, even to the phrases of it, out of the
writings of Salmasius against Milton, but which is really
only to be paralleled by the much worse language of
Milton against Salmasius.   It was in truth exactly the kind
of incensed speech which, at a later date, the factions in
Paris levelled against one another, when Girondins screamed
for the heads of Jacobins, and Robespierre denounced
Danton, and Tallien cried for the blood of Robespierre.

Burke declined most wisely to suggest any plan for the
National Assembly.   "Permit me to say,"—this is in the
letter of January, 1791, to a member of the Assembly,—
" that if I were as confident as I ought to be diffident in
my own loose general ideas, I never should venture to
broach them, if but at twenty leagues' distance from the
centre of your affairs.   I must see with my own eyes; I
must in a manner touch with my own hands, not only the
fixed, but momentary circumstances, before I could venture
to suggest any political project whatsoever.   I must know
the power and disposition to accept, to execute, to persevere.
I must see all the aids and all the obstacles.   I must see

the means of correcting the plan, where correctives would
be wanted. I must see the things : I must see the men.
Without a concurrence and adaptation of these to the
design, the very best speculative projects might become
not only useless but mischievous. Plans must be made
for men. People at a distance must judge ill of men.
They do not always answer to their reputation when you
approach them. Nay, the perspective varies, and shows
them quite other than you thought them. At a distance,
if we judge uncertainly of men, we must judge worse of
opportunities, which continually vary their shapes and
colours, and pass away like clouds." Our admiration at
such words is quickly stifled when we recall the confident,
unsparing, immoderate criticism which both preceded and
followed this truly rational exposition of the danger of
advising, in cases where we know neither the men nor
the opportunities. Why was savage and unfaltering
denunciation any less unbecoming than, as he admits,
crude prescriptions would have been unbecoming ?

By the end of 1791, when he wrote the *Thoughts on
French Affairs*, he had penetrated still further into the
essential character of the Revolution. Any notion of a
reform to be effected after the decorous pattern of 1688,
so conspicuous in the first great manifesto, had wholly
disappeared. The changes in France he allowed to bear
little resemblance or analogy to any of those which had
been previously brought about in Europe. It is a revolution, he said, of doctrine and theoretic dogma. The
Reformation was the last revolution of this sort which
had happened in Europe ; and he immediately goes on to
remark a point of striking resemblance between them.
The effect of the Reformation was "to introduce other
interests into all countries than those which arose from

their locality and natural circumstances." In like manner
other sources of faction were now opened, combining
parties among the inhabitants of different countries into
a single connection. From these sources, effects were
likely to arise fully as important as those which had
formerly arisen from the jarring interests of the religious
sects. It is a species of faction which "breaks the locality
of public affections."[1]

He was thus launched on the full tide of his policy.
The French Revolution must be hemmed in by a cordon
of fire. Those who sympathised with it in England
must be gagged, and if gagging did not suffice, they must
be taught respect for the constitution in dungeons and
on the gallows. His cry for war abroad and arbitrary
tyranny at home waxed louder every day. As Fox said,
it was lucky that Burke took the royal side in the Revolution, for his violence would certainly have got him
hanged if he had happened to take the other side.

It was in the early summer of 1792 that Miss Burney
again met Burke at Mrs. Crewe's villa at Hampstead.
He entered into an animated conversation on Lord
Macartney and the Chinese expedition, reviving all the
old enthusiasm of his companion by his allusions and
anecdotes, his brilliant fancies and wide information.
When politics were introduced, he spoke with an eager-

---

[1] De Tocqueville has unconsciously imitated Burke's very
phrases. "Toutes les révolutions civiles et politiques ont eu une
patrie, et s'y sont enfermées. La Révolution française . . . on
l'a vue rapprocher ou diviser les hommes en dépit des lois, des traditions des caractères, de langue, rendant parfois ennemis des
compatriotes, et frères des étrangers ; *ou plutôt elle a formé au-
dessus de toutes les nationalités particulières, une patrie intellec-
tuelle commune dont les hommes de toutes les nations ont pu devenir
citoyens.*"—Ancien Régime, p. 15.

ness and a vehemence that instantly banished the graces,
though it redoubled the energies of his discourse. "How
I wish," Miss Burney writes, "that you could meet this
wonderful man when he is easy, happy, and with people
he cordially likes. But politics, even on his own side,
must always be excluded ; his irritability is so terrible
on that theme, that it gives immediately to his face *the
expression of a man who is going to defend himself from
murderers.*"

Burke still remained without a following, but the ranks
of his old allies gradually began to show signs of waver-
ing. His panic about the Jacobins within the gates slowly
spread. His old faith, about which he had once talked so
much, in the ancient rustic, manly, home-bred sense of the
English people, he dismissed as if it had been some idle dream
that had come to him through the ivory gate. His fine
comparison of the nation to a majestic herd, browsing in
peace amid the importunate chirrupings of a thousand
crickets, became so little appropriate, that he was now
beside himself with apprehension that the crickets were
about to rend the oxen in pieces. Even then, the herd
stood tranquilly in their pastures, only occasionally
turning a dull eye, now to France, and now to Burke. In
the autumn of 1791, Burke dined with Pitt and Lord
Grenville, and he found them resolute for an honest
neutrality in the affairs of France, and "quite out of all
apprehensions of any effect from the French Revolution in
this kingdom, either at present or any time to come."
Francis and Sheridan, it is true, spoke as if they almost
wished for a domestic convulsion ; and cool observers who
saw him daily, even accused Sheridan of wishing to stir up
the lower ranks of the people by the hope of plundering
their betters. But men who afterwards became alarmists,

are found, so late as the spring of 1792, declaring in their
most confidential correspondence that the party of confusion made no way with the country, and produced no
effect.   Horne Tooke was its most conspicuous chief, and
nobody pretended to fear the subversion of the realm by
Horne Tooke.   Yet Burke, in letters where he admits
that the democratic party is entirely discountenanced,
and that the Jacobin faction in England is under a
heavy cloud, was so possessed by the spectre of panic,
as to declare that the Duke of Brunswick was as much
fighting the battle of the crown of England, as the Duke
of Cumberland fought that battle at Culloden.

Time and events, meanwhile, had been powerfully telling
for Burke.   While he was writing his *Appeal*, the French
King and Queen had destroyed whatever confidence sanguine
dreamers might have had in their loyalty to the new order
of things, by attempting to escape over the frontier.   They
were brought back, and a manful attempt was made to get
the new constitution to work, in the winter of 1791–92.
It was soon found out that Mirabeau had been right, when
he said that for a monarchy it was too democratic, and for
a republic there was a king too much.   This was Burke's
Reflections in a nutshell.   But it was foreign intervention
that finally ruined the King, and destroyed the hope of an
orderly issue.   Frederick the Great had set the first example of what some call iniquity and violence in Europe,
and others in milder terms call a readjustment of the
equilibrium of nations.   He had taken Silesia from the
house of Austria, and he had shared in the first partition
of Poland.   Catherine II. had followed him at the expense
of Poland, Sweden, and Turkey.   However we may view
these transactions, and whether we describe them by the
stern words of the moralist, or the more deprecatory

words of the diplomatist, they are the first sources of that
storm of lawless rapine which swept over every part of
Europe for five-and-twenty years to come.   The intervention of Austria and Prussia in the affairs of France was
originally less a deliberate design for the benefit of the old
order, than an interlude in the intrigues of eastern Europe.
But the first effect of intervention on behalf of the French
monarchy was to bring it in a few weeks to the ground.

    In the spring of 1792 France replied to the preparations
of Austria and Prussia for invasion, by a declaration of
war.   It was inevitable that the French people should
associate the court with the foreign enemy that was
coming to its deliverance.   Everybody knew as well then
as we know it now, that the Queen was as bitterly incensed against the new order of things, and as resolutely
unfaithful to it, as the most furious emigrant on the
Rhine.   Even Burke himself, writing to his son at
Coblenz, was constrained to talk about Marie Antoinette
as that "most unfortunate woman, who was not to be
cured of the spirit of court intrigue even by a prison."
The King may have been loyally resigned to his position,
but resignation will not defend a country from the invader ;
and the nation distrusted a chief who only a few months
before had been arrested in full flight to join the national
enemy.   Power naturally fell into the hands of the men
of conviction, energy, passion, and resource.   Patriotism
and republicanism became synonymous, and the constitution against which Burke had prophesied, was henceforth a dead letter.   The spirit of insurrection that had
slumbered since the fall of the Bastille and the march to
Versailles in 1789, now awoke in formidable violence,
and after the preliminary rehearsal of what is known in
the revolutionary calendar as the 20th of June (1792),

IX.]   THE FRENCH KING'S DEATH.   191

the people of Paris responded to the Duke of Brunswick's insensate manifesto by the more memorable day of
the 10th of August. Brunswick, accepting the hateful
language which the French emigrants put into his mouth,
had declared that every member of the national guard
taken with arms in his hands would be immediately put
to death; that every inhabitant who should dare to defend
himself, would be put to death and his house burnt to
the ground; and that if the least insult was offered to
the royal family, then their Austrian and Prussian majes-
ties would deliver Paris to military execution and total
destruction. This is the vindictive ferocity which only
civil war can kindle. To convince men that the manifesto was not an empty threat, on the day of its publication a force of nearly 140,000 Austrians, Prussians, and
Hessians entered France. The sections of Paris replied
by marching to the Tuileries, and after a furious conflict
with the Swiss guards, they stormed the chateau. The
King and his family had fled to the National Assembly.
The same evening they were thrown into prison, whence
the King and Queen only came out on their way to the
scaffold.

It was the King's execution in January, 1793, that
finally raised feeling in England to the intense heat which
Burke had for so long been craving. The evening on
which the courier brought the news was never forgotten
by those who were in London at the time. The play-
houses were instantly closed, and the audiences insisted
on retiring with half the amusement for which they had
paid. People of the lowest and the highest rank alike
put on mourning. The French were universally denounced
as fiends upon earth. It was hardly safe for a Frenchman
to appear in the streets of London. Placards were posted

on every wall, calling for war, and the crowds who gathered round them, read them with loud hurrahs.

It would be a great mistake to say that Pitt ever lost his head, but he lost his feet. The momentary passion of the nation forced him out of the pacific path in which he would have chosen to stay. Burke had become the greatest power in the country, and was in closer communication with the ministers than any one out of office. He went once about this time with Windham and Elliot, to inform Pitt as to the uneasiness of the public about the slackness of our naval and military preparation. "Burke," says one of the party, "gave Pitt a little political instruction in a very respectful and cordial way, but with the authority of an old and most informed statesman, and although nobody ever takes the whole of Burke's advice, yet he often, or always rather, furnishes very important and useful matter, some part of which sticks and does good. Pitt took it all very patiently and cordially."

It was in the December of 1792 that Burke had enacted that famous bit of melodrama out of place, known as the Dagger Scene. The government had brought in an Alien Bill, imposing certain pains and restrictions on foreigners coming to this country. Fox denounced it as a concession to foolish alarms, and was followed by Burke, who began to storm as usual against murderous atheists. Then without due preparation he began to fumble in his bosom, suddenly drew out a dagger, and with an extravagant gesture, threw it on the floor of the House, crying that this was what they had to expect from their alliance with France. The stroke missed its mark, and there was a general inclination to titter, until Burke, collecting him-

self for an effort, called upon them with a vehemence to
which his listeners could not choose but respond, to keep
French principles from their heads, and French daggers
from their hearts; to preserve all their blandishments in
life, and all their consolations in death; all the blessings
of time, and all the hopes of eternity. All this was not
prepared long beforehand, for it seems that the dagger had
only been shown to Burke on his way to the House, as
one that had been sent to Birmingham to be a pattern
for a large order. Whether prepared or unprepared,
the scene was one from which we gladly avert our eyes.

Negotiations had been going on for some months, and
they continued in various stages for some months longer,
for a coalition between the two great parties of the state.
Burke was persistently anxious that Fox should join Pitt's
government. Pitt always admitted the importance of
Fox's abilities in the difficult affairs which lay before the
ministry, and declared that he had no sort of personal
animosity to Fox, but rather a personal good-will and
good-liking. Fox himself said of a coalition, " It is so
damned right, to be sure, that I cannot help thinking it
must be." But the difficulties were insuperable. The
more rapidly the government drifted in Burke's direction,
the more impossible was it for a man of Fox's political
sympathies and convictions to have any dealings with a
cabinet committed to a policy of irrational panic, to be
carried out by a costly war abroad and cruel repression at
home. " *What a very wretched man!* " was Burke's angry
exclamation one day, when it became certain that Fox
meant to stand by the old flag of freedom and generous
common sense.

When the coalition at length took place (1794), the
only man who carried Burke's principles to their fullest

extent into Pitt's cabinet, was Windham.   It is impossible
not to feel the attraction of Windham's character, his
amiability, his reverence for great and virtuous men, his
passion for knowledge, the versatility of his interests.   He
is a striking example of the fact that literature was a common
pursuit and occupation to the chief statesmen of that time
(always excepting Pitt), to an extent that has been gradually
tending to become rarer.   Windham, in the midst of his
devotion to public affairs, to the business of his country,
and, let us add, a zealous attendance on every prize fight
within reach, was never happy unless he was working up
points in literature and mathematics.   There was a literary
and classical spirit abroad, and in spite of the furious pre-
occupations of faction, a certain ready disengagement of
mind prevailed.   If Windham and Fox began to talk of
horses, they seemed to fall naturally into what had been said
about horses by the old writers.   Fox held that long ears
were a merit, and Windham met him by the authority of
Xenophon and Oppian in favour of short ones, and finally
they went off into what it was that Virgil meant, when he
called a horse's head *argutum caput*.   Burke and Windham
travelled in Scotland together in 1785, and their conversation fell as often on old books, as on Hastings or on Pitt.
They discussed Virgil's similes ; Johnson and L'Estrange,
as the extremes of English style ; what Stephens and A.
Gellius had to say about Cicero's use of the word *gratiosus*.
If they came to libraries, Windham ran into them with
eagerness, and very strongly enjoyed all " the *feel* that a
library usually excites."   He is constantly reproaching
himself with a remissness, which was purely imaginary, in
keeping up his mathematics, his Greek tragedies, his
Latin historians.   There is no more curious example of
the remorse of a bookman impeded by affairs.   " What

progress might men make in the several parts of knowledge," he says very truly, in one of these moods, " if they
could only pursue them with the same eagerness and
assiduity as are exerted by lawyers in the conduct of a
suit." But this distraction between the tastes of the book-
man and the pursuits of public business, united with a
certain quality of his constitution to produce one great
defect in his character, and it was the worst defect that a
statesman can have. He became the most irresolute and
vacillating of men. He wastes the first half of a day in
deciding which of two courses to take, and the second half
in blaming himself for not having taken the other. He
is constantly late at entertainments, because he cannot
make up his mind in proper time whether to go or to stay
at home; hesitation whether he shall read in the red
room or in the library, loses him three of the best hours of
a morning; the difficulty of early rising he finds to consist less in rising early, than in satisfying himself that
the practice is wholesome; his mind is torn for a whole fore-
noon in an absurd contest with himself, whether he ought to
indulge a strong wish to exercise his horse before dinner.
Every page of his diary is a register of the symptoms of
this unhappy disease. When the Revolution came, he
was absolutely forced by the iron necessity of the case,
after certain perturbations, to go either with Fox or with
Burke. Under this compulsion he took one headlong
plunge into the policy of alarm. Everybody knows how
desperately an habitually irresolute man is capable of cling-
ing to a policy or a conviction, to which he has once
been driven by dire stress of circumstance. Windham
having at last made up his mind to be frightened by the
Revolution, was more violently and inconsolably frightened
than anybody else.

Pitt, after he had been forced into war, at least intended it to be a war on the good old-fashioned principles of seizing the enemy's colonies and keeping them. He was taunted by the alarmists with caring only for sugar islands, and making himself master of all the islands in the world except Great Britain and Ireland. To Burke all this was an abomination, and Windham followed Burke to the letter. He even declared the holy rage of the *Fourth Letter on a Regicide Peace*, published after Burke's death, to contain the purest wisdom and the most unanswerable policy. It was through Windham's eloquence and perseverance that the monstrous idea of a crusade, and all Burke's other violent and excited precepts, gained an effective place and hearing in the cabinet, in the royal closet, and in the House of Commons, long after Burke himself had left the scene.

We have already seen how important an element Irish affairs became in the war with America. The same spirit which had been stirred by the American war, was inevitably kindled in Ireland by the French Revolution. The association of United Irishmen now came into existence, with aims avowedly revolutionary. They joined the party which was striving for the relief of the Catholics from certain disabilities, and for their admission to the franchise. Burke had watched all movements in his native country, from the Whiteboy insurrection of 1761 downwards, with steady vigilance, and he watched the new movement of 1792 with the keenest eyes. It made him profoundly uneasy. He could not endure the thought of ever so momentary and indirect an association with a revolutionary party, either in Ireland or any other quarter of the globe, yet he was eager for a policy which should reconcile the Irish. He was so for two reasons. One of

them was his political sense of the inexpediency of pro-
scribing men by whole nations, and excluding from the
franchise on the ground of religion a people as numerous
as the subjects of the King of Denmark or the King of
Sardinia, equal to the population of the United Nether-
lands, and larger than were to be found in all the States
of Switzerland. His second reason was his sense of the
urgency of facing trouble abroad with a nation united and
contented at home; of abolishing in the heart of the
country that "bank of discontent, every hour accumu-
lating, upon which every description of seditious men
may draw at pleasure."

In the beginning of 1792, Burke's son went to
Dublin as the agent and adviser of the Catholic Committee, who at first listened to him with the respect due
to one in whom they expected to find the qualities of his
father. They soon found out that he was utterly without
either tact or judgment; that he was arrogant, im-
pertinent, vain, and empty. Wolfe Tone declared him
to be by far the most impudent and opinionative fellow
that he had ever known in his life. Nothing could exceed
the absurdity of his conduct, and on one occasion he had
a very narrow escape of being taken into custody by the
Serjeant-at-arms, for rushing down from the gallery into the
Irish House of Commons, and attempting to make a speech
in defence of a petition which he had drawn up, and
which was being attacked by a member in his place.
Richard Burke went home, it is said, with two thousand
guineas in his pocket, which the Catholics had cheerfully
paid as the price of getting rid of him. He returned
shortly after, but only helped to plunge the business into
further confusion, and finally left the scene covered with
odium and discredit. His father's *Letter to Sir Hercules*

Langrishe (1792) remains an admirable monument of wise
statesmanship, a singular interlude of calm and solid
reasoning in the midst of a fiery whirlwind of intense
passion. Burke perhaps felt that the state of Ireland was
passing away from the sphere of calm and solid reason,
when he knew that Dumouriez's victory over the allies at
Valmy, which filled Beaconsfield with such gloom and
dismay, was celebrated at Dublin by an illumination.

Burke, who was now in his sixty-fourth year, had for
some time announced his intention of leaving the House
of Commons, as soon as he had brought to an end the
prosecution of Hastings. In 1794 the trial came to a
close; the thanks of the House were formally voted to
the managers of the impeachment; and when the scene
was over, Burke applied for the Chiltern Hundreds. Lord
Fitzwilliam nominated Richard Burke for the seat which
his father had thus vacated at Malton. Pitt was
then making arrangements for the accession of the
Portland Whigs to his government, and it was natural,
in connexion with these arrangements, to confer some
favour on the man who had done more than anybody
else to promote the new alliance. It was proposed to
make Burke a peer under the style of Lord Beaconsfield,—
a title in a later age whimsically borrowed for himself by
a man of genius who delighted in irony. To the title it
was proposed to attach a yearly income for two or more
lives. But the bolt of destiny was at this instant
launched. Richard Burke, the adored centre of all his
father's hopes and affections, was seized with illness, and
died (August, 1794). We cannot look without tragic
emotion on the pathos of the scene, which left the rem-
nant of the old man's days desolate and void. A Roman
poet has described in touching words the woe of the aged

Nestor, as he beheld the funeral pile of his son, too un-
timely slain,—

" Oro parumper
Attendas quantum de legibus ipse queratur
Fatorum et nimio de stamine, quum videt acris
Antilochi barbam ardentem : quum quærit ab omni
Quisquis adest socius, cur hæc in tempora duret,
Quod facinus dignum tam longo admiserit ævo."

Burke's grief finds a nobler expression. "The storm
has gone over me, and I lie like one of those old oaks
which the late hurricane has scattered about me. I am
stripped of all my honours ; I am torn up by the roots and
lie prostrate on the earth. . . I am alone. I have
none to meet my enemies in the gate. . . I live in an
inverted order. They who ought to have succeeded me
have gone before me. They who should have been to me
as posterity, are in the place of ancestors."

Burke only lived three years after this desolating blow.
The arrangements for a peerage, as a matter of course,
came to an end. But Pitt was well aware of the serious embarrassments by which Burke was so pressed that he saw
actual beggary very close at hand. The King, too,—who had
once, by the way, granted a pension to Burke's detested
Rousseau, though Rousseau was too proud to draw it—
seems to have been honourably interested in making a
provision for Burke. What Pitt offered was an immediate grant of 1200*l.* a year from the Civil List for Mrs.
Burke's life, to be followed by a proposition to Parliament
in a message from the king, to confer an annuity of greater
value upon a statesman who had served the country to his
own loss for thirty years. As a matter of fact, the grant,
2500*l.* a year in amount, much to Burke's chagrin, was
never brought before Parliament, but was conferred directly

by the Crown, as a charge on a certain stock known as
the West India four-and-a-half per cents. It seems as it
Pitt were afraid of challenging the opinion of Parliament ;
and the storm which the pension raised out of doors, was
a measure of the trouble which the defence of it would
have inflicted on the government inside the House of
Commons. According to the rumour of the time, Burke
sold two of his pensions upon lives for 27,000*l.*, and there
was left the third pension of 1200*l.* for his wife's life. By-
and-by, when the resentment of the Opposition was
roused to the highest pitch by the infamous Treason and
Sedition Bills of 1795, the Duke of Bedford and Lord
Lauderdale, seeking to accumulate every possible complaint
against the government, assailed the grant to Burke, as
made without the consent of Parliament, and as a violent
contradiction to the whole policy of the plan for
economic reform. The attack, if not unjustifiable in itself,
came from an unlucky quarter. A chief of the house of
Bedford was the most unfit person in the world to protest
against grants by favour of the Crown. Burke was too
practised a rhetorician not to see the opening, and his
Letter to a Noble Lord is the most splendid repartee in
the English language.

It is not surprising that Burke's defence should have
provoked rejoinder. A cloud of pamphlets followed the
Letter to a Noble Lord—some in doggrel verse, others
in a magniloquent prose imitated from his own, others,
mere poisonous scurrility. The nearest approach to a
just stroke that I can find, after turning over a pile of this
trash, is an expression of wonder that he, who was incon-
solable for the loss of a beloved son, should not have reflected how many tender parents had been made childless in
the profusion of blood, of which he himself had been the

most relentless champion. Our disgust at the pages of
insult which were here levelled at a great man, is perhaps
moderated by the thought that Burke himself, who of all
people ought to have known better, had held up to public
scorn and obloquy men of such virtue, attainments, and
real service to mankind, as Richard Price and Joseph
Priestley.

It was during these months that he composed the *Letters
on a Regicide Peace*, though the third and fourth of them
were not published until after his death. There have been
those to whom these compositions appeared to be Burke's
masterpieces. In fact they are deplorable. They contain
passages of fine philosophy and of skilful and plausible
reasoning, but such passages only make us wonder how
they come to be where they are. The reader is in no
humour for them. In splendour of rhetoric, in fine images,
in sustention, in irony, they surpass anything that Burke
ever wrote, but of the qualities and principles that, far
more than his rhetoric, have made Burke so admirable and
so great—of justice, of firm grasp of fact, of a reasonable
sense of the probabilities of things—there are only traces
enough to light up the gulfs of empty words, reckless
phrases, and senseless vituperations, that surge and boil
around them.

It is with the same emotion of "grief and shame" with
which Fox heard Burke argue against relief to Dissenters,
that we hear him abusing the courts of law because they
did not convict Hardy and Horne Tooke. The pages
against divorce and civil marriage, even granting that they
point to the right judgment in these matters, express it
with a vehemence that is irrational, and in the dialect,
not of a statesman, but of an enraged Capucin. The highly
wrought passage in which Burke describes external aggran-

disement as the original thought and the ultimate aim of
the earlier statesmen of the Revolution, is no better than
ingenious nonsense. The whole performance rests on a
gross and inexcusable anachronism. There is a con-
temptuous refusal to discriminate between groups of men
who were as different from one another as Oliver Cromwell was different from James Nayler, and between periods
which were as unlike in all their conditions as the Athens of
the Thirty Tyrants was unlike Athens after Thrasybulus
had driven the Tyrants out. He assumes that the men,
the policy, the maxims of the French government are the
men, the policy, and the maxims of the handful of obscure
miscreants who had hacked priests and nobles to pieces at
the doors of the prisons four years before. Carnot is to
him merely " that sanguinary tyrant," and the heroic
Hoche becomes " that old practised assassin," while the
Prince of Wales, by the way, and the Duke of York are
the hope and pride of nations. To heap up that incessant
iteration about thieves, murderers, housebreakers, assassins,
bandits, bravoes with their hands dripping with blood and
their maw gorged with property, desperate paramours, bom-
bastical players, the refuse and rejected offal of strolling
theatres, bloody buffoons, bloody felons—all this was as
unjust to hundreds of disinterested, honest, and patriotic
men who were then earnestly striving to restore a true
order and solid citizenship in France, as the foul-mouthed
scurrility of an Irish Orangeman is unjust to millions of
devout Catholics.

Burke was the man who might have been expected before all others to know that in every system of government,
whatever may have been the crimes of its origin, there is
sure, by the bare necessity of things, to rise up a party or
an individual, whom their political instinct will force

into resistance to the fatalities of anarchy. Man is
too strongly a political animal for it to be otherwise.
It was so at each period and division in the Revolution. There was always a party of order, and by 1796,
when Burke penned these reckless philippics, order
was only too easy in France. The Revolution had worn
out the passion and moral enthusiasm of its first years,
and all the best men of the revolutionary time had
been consumed in a flame of fire. When Burke talked
about this war being wholly unlike any war that ever was
waged in Europe before, about its being a war for
justice on the one side, and a fanatical bloody propa-
gandism on the other, he shut his eyes to the plain fact
that the Directory had after all really sunk to the moral
level of Frederick and Catherine, or for that matter, of
Louis the Fourteenth himself. This war was only too like
the other great wars of European history. The French
government had become political, exactly in the same sense
in which Thugut and Metternich and Herzberg were political. The French Republic in 1797 was neither more nor
less aggressive, immoral, piratical, than the monarchies
which had partitioned Poland, and had intended to redis-
tribute the continent of Europe to suit their own ambitions. The Coalition began the game, but France
proved too strong for them, and they had the worst of
their game. Jacobinism may have inspired the original fire
which made her armies irresistible, but Jacobinism of that
stamp had now gone out of fashion, and to denounce a
peace with the Directory because the origin of their
government was regicidal, was as childish as it would
have been in Mazarin to decline a treaty of regicide peace
with Oliver Cromwell.

What makes the *Regicide Peace* so repulsive is not that

it recommends energetic prosecution of the war, and not
that it abounds in glaring fallacies in detail, but that it is
in direct contradiction with that strong, positive, rational,
and sane method which had before uniformly marked
Burke's political philosophy.   Here lay his inconsistency,
not in abandoning democratic principles, for he had never
held them, but in forgetting his own rules, that nations
act from adequate motives relative to their interests, and
not from metaphysical speculation ; that we cannot draw
an indictment against a whole people, that there is a
species of hostile justice which no asperity of war wholly
extinguishes in the minds of a civilized people.   " Steady
independent minds " he had once said, " when they have
an object of so serious a concern to mankind as *government* under their contemplation, will disdain to assume
the part of satirists and declaimers."   Show the thing
that you ask for, he cried during the American war,
to be reason, show it to be common sense.   We have a
measure of the reason and common sense of Burke's
attitude in the *Regicide Peace*, in the language which it
inspired in Windham and others, who denounced Wilberforce for canting when he spoke of peace ; who stigmatized
Pitt as weak and a pander to national avarice for thinking
of the cost of the war ; and who actually charged the
liverymen of London who petitioned for peace, with open
sedition.

It is a striking illustration of the versatility of Burke's
moods, that immediately before sitting down to write the
flaming *Letters on a Regicide Peace*, he had composed
one of the most lucid and accurately meditated of all
of his tracts, which, short as it is, contains ideas on
free trade which was only too far in advance of the
opinion of his time.   In 1772 a Corn Bill had been
introduced—it was passed in the following year—of which

Adam Smith said, that it was like the laws of Solon, not
the best in itself, but the best which the situation and
tendency of the times would admit. In speaking upon
this measure, Burke had laid down those sensible principles on the trade in corn, which he now in 1795
worked out in the *Thoughts and Details on Scarcity*.
Those who do not concern themselves with economics
will perhaps be interested in the singular passage, vigor-
ously objected to by Dugald Stewart, in which Burke sets
up a genial defence of the consumption of ardent spirits.
It is interesting as an argument, and it is most characteristic of the author.

The curtain was now falling. All who saw him, felt
that Burke's life was quickly drawing to a close. His
son's death had struck the final blow. We could only
wish that the years had brought to him, what it ought to
be the fervent prayer of us all to find at the close of the
long struggle with ourselves and with circumstance,—a
disposition to happiness, a composed spirit to which time
has made things clear, an unrebellious temper, and hopes
undimmed for mankind. If this was not so, Burke at least
busied himself to the end in great interests. His charity
to the unfortunate emigrants from France was diligent
and unwearied. Among other solid services, he established a school at Beaconsfield for sixty French boys,
principally the orphans of Quiberon, and the children of
other emigrants who had suffered in the cause. Almost
the last glimpse that we have of Burke, is in a record of a
visit to Beaconsfield by the author of the *Vindiciæ Gallicæ*.
Mackintosh had written to Burke, to express his admiration for his character and genius, and recanting his old
defence of the Revolution. "Since that time," he said,
"a melancholy experience has undeceived me on many
subjects, in which I was then the dupe of my enthusiasm."

When Mackintosh went to Beaconsfield (Christmas, 1797),
he was as much amazed as every one else with the exube-
rance of his host's mind in conversation. Even then Burke
entered with cordial glee into the sports of children, rolling
about with them on the carpet, and pouring out in his
gambols the sublimest images, mixed with the most
wretched puns. He said of Fox, with a deep sigh, "He
is made to be loved." There was the irresistible outbreak
against "that putrid carcase, that mother of all evil—the
French Revolution." It reminded him of the accursed
things that crawled in and out of the mouth of the vile
hag in Spenser's Cave of Error; and he repeated the
nauseous stanza. Mackintosh was to be the faithful
knight of the romance, the brightness of whose sword
was to flash destruction on the filthy progeny.

It was on the 9th of July, 1797, that in the sixty-eighth
year of his age, preserving his faculties to the last moment,
he expired. With magnanimous tenderness, Fox proposed that he should be buried among the great dead in
Westminster Abbey; but Burke had left strict injunc-
tions that his funeral should be private, and he was laid
in the little church at Beaconsfield. It was a terrible
moment in the history of England and of Europe. An
open mutiny had just been quelled in the fleet. There
had been signs of disaffection in the army. In Ireland
the spirit of revolt was smouldering, which in a few
months broke out in the fierce flames of a great rebellion.
And it was the year of the political crime of Campo
Formio, that sinister pacification in which violence
and fraud once more asserted their unveiled ascendancy
in Europe. These sombre shadows were falling over the
western world, when a life went out, which, notwith-
standing some grave aberrations, had made great tides
in human destiny very luminous.

CHAPTER X.

A STORY is told that in the time when Burke was still at peace with the Dissenters, he visited Priestley, and after seeing his library and his laboratory, and hearing how his host's hours were given to experiment and meditation, he exclaimed that such a life must make him the happiest and most to be envied of men. It must sometimes have occurred to Burke to wonder whether he had made the right choice when he locked away the fragments of his history, and plunged into the torment of party and Parliament. But his interests and aptitudes were too strong and overmastering for him to have been right in doing otherwise. Contact with affairs was an indispensable condition for the full use of his great faculties, in spite of their being less faculties of affairs than of speculation. Public life was the actual field in which to test, and work out, and use with good effect the moral ideas which were Burke's most sincere and genuine interests. And he was able to bring these moral ideas into such effective use because he was so entirely unfettered by the narrowing spirit of formula. No man, for instance, who thought in formulæ would have written the curious passage that I have already referred to, in which he eulogises gin, because "under the pressure of the cares and sorrows of our mortal condition, men have at all times and in all countries called in some physical aid to their moral consolation." He valued words at their proper rate, that is to say, he knew that some of the greatest facts in the life and character of man, and in the institutions of society, can find no description and no measurement in words. Public life, as we can easily perceive, with its shibboleths, its exclusive parties, its measurement by conventional standards, its attention to small expediencies before the larger ones, is not a field where such characteristics are likely to make an instant effect.

Though it is not wrong to say of Burke that, as an orator, he was transcendent, yet in that immediate influence upon his hearers which is commonly supposed to be the mark of oratorical success, all the evidence is that Burke generally failed. We have seen how his speech against Hastings affected Miss Burney, and how the speech on the Nabob of Arcot's debts was judged by Pitt not to be worth answering. Perhaps the greatest that he ever made was that on conciliation with America; the wisest in its temper, the most closely logical in its reasoning, the amplest in appropriate topics, the most generous and conciliatory in the substance of its appeals. Yet Erskine, who was in the House when this was delivered, said that it drove everybody away, including people who, when they came to read it, read it over and over again and could hardly think of anything else. As Moore says rather too floridly, but with truth,—" In vain did Burke's genius put forth its superb plumage, glittering all over with the hundred eyes of fancy—the gait of the bird was heavy and awkward, and its voice seemed rather to scare than attract." Burke's gestures were clumsy; he had sonorous but harsh tones; he never lost a strong Irish accent; and his utterance was often hurried and eager. Apart from these disadvantages of accident which have been overcome by men infinitely inferior to Burke, it is easy to perceive, from the matter and texture of the speeches that have become English classics, that the very qualities which are excellences in literature were draw-backs to the spoken discourses. A listener in Westminster Hall or the House of Commons, unlike the reader by his fireside in the next century, is always thinking of argu-ments and facts that bear directly on the special issue before him. What he wishes to hear is some particularity of event or inference which will either help him to make up his mind, or will justify him if his mind is already made up. Burke never neglected these particularities, and he never went so wide as to fall for an instant into vagueness, but he went wide enough into the generalities that lent force and light to his view, to weary men who cared for nothing, and could not be expected to care for anything, but the business actually in hand and the most expeditious way through it. The contentiousness is not close enough and rapid enough to hold the interest of a practical assembly, which, though it was a hundred times less busy than the House of Commons to-day, seems to have been eager in the inverse proportion of what it had to do, to get that little quickly done.

Then we may doubt whether there is any instance of an orator throwing his spell over a large audience, without frequent resort to the higher forms of commonplace. Two of the greatest speeches of Burke's time are supposed to have been Grattan's on Tithes and Fox's on the West-minster Scrutiny, and these were evidently full of the splendid commonplaces of the first-rate rhetorician. Burke's mind was not readily set to these tunes. The emotion to

P

which he commonly appealed was that too rare one, the
love of wisdom, and he combined his thoughts and knowledge in propositions of wisdom so weighty and strong,
that the minds of ordinary hearers were not on the instant
prepared for them.

It is true that Burke's speeches were not without effect
of an indirect kind, for there is good evidence that at
the time when Lord North's ministry was tottering,
Burke had risen to a position of the first eminence in
Parliament.   When Boswell said to him that people
would wonder how he could bring himself to take so much
pains with his speeches, knowing with certainty that not
one vote would be gained by them, Burke answered that
it is very well worth while to take pains to speak well in
Parliament; for if a man speaks well, he gradually estab-
lishes a certain reputation and consequence in the general
opinion; and though an Act that has been ably opposed
becomes law, yet in its progress it is softened and modified
to meet objections whose force has never been acknowledged
directly.   " Aye, sir," Johnson broke in, "and there is
a gratification of pride.   Though we cannot out-vote them,
we will out-argue them."

Out-arguing is not perhaps the right word for most of
Burke's performances. He is at heart thinking more of
the subject itself, than of those on whom it was his apparent business to impress a particular view of it. He
surrenders himself wholly to the matter, and follows up,
though with a strong and close tread, all the excursions to
which it may give rise in an elastic intelligence—" motion,"
as De Quincey says, " propagating motion, and life
throwing off life."   But then this exuberant way of thinking, this willingness to let the subject lead, is less apt in
public discourse than it is in literature, and from this comes
the literary quality of Burke's speeches.

With all his hatred for the book-man in politics, Burke
owed much of his own distinction to that generous rich-
ness and breadth of judgment which had been ripened in
him by literature and his practice in it. Like some other
men in our history, he showed that books are a better
preparation for statesmanship, than early training in the
subordinate posts and among the permanent officials of a
public department. There is no copiousness of literary
reference in his works, such as over-abounded in civil and
ecclesiastical publicists of the seventeenth century. Nor
can we truly say that there is much, though there is certainly
some, of that tact, which literature is alleged to confer on
those who approach it in a just spirit and with the true
gift. The influence of literature on Burke lay partly in the
direction of emancipation from the mechanical formulæ of
practical politics; partly in the association which it engendered, in a powerful understanding like his, between
politics and the moral forces of the world, and between
political maxims and the old and great sentences of morals;
partly in drawing him, even when resting his case on
prudence and expediency, to appeal to the widest and
highest sympathies; partly, and more than all, in opening
his thoughts to the many conditions, possibilities, and
" varieties of untried being " in human character and
situation, and so giving an incomparable flexibility to his
methods of political approach.

This flexibility is not to be found in his manner and
composition. That derives its immense power from other
sources; from passion, intensity, imagination, size, truth,
cogency of logical reason. If any one has imbued himself
with that exacting love of delicacy, measure, and taste in
expression, which was until our own day a sacred tradition of
the French, then he will not like Burke. Those who insist on

charm, on winningness in style, on subtle harmonies and
exquisite suggestion, are disappointed in Burke ; they even
find him stiff and over-coloured.   And there are blemishes
of this kind.   His banter is nearly always ungainly, his wit
blunt, as Johnson said of it, and very often unseasonable.
We feel that Johnson must have been right in declaring
that though Burke was always in search of pleasantries,
he never made a good joke in his life.   As is usual with
a man who has not true humour, Burke is also without
true pathos.   The thought of wrong or misery moved
him less to pity for the victim, than to anger against
the cause.   Again, there are some gratuitous and un-
redeemed vulgarities ; some images whose barbarity makes
us shudder, of creeping ascarides and inexpugnable tape-
worms.   But it is the mere foppery of literature to suffer
ourselves to be long detained by specks like these.

The varieties of Burke's literary or rhetorical method
are very striking.   It is almost incredible that the superb
imaginative amplification of the description of Hyder Ali's
descent upon the Carnatic should be from the same pen as
the grave, simple, unadorned *Address to the King* (1777),
where each sentence falls on the ear with the accent of
some golden-tongued oracle of the wise gods.   His stride
is the stride of a giant, from the sentimental beauty of
the picture of Marie Antoinette at Versailles, or the red
horror of the tale of Debi Sing in Rungpore, to the learning, positiveness, and cool judicial mastery of the *Report
on the Lords' Journals* (1794), which Philip Francis, no
mean judge, declared on the whole to be the " most eminent and extraordinary " of all his productions.   Even in
the coolest and dryest of his pieces, there is the mark of
greatness, of grasp, of comprehension.   In all its varieties
Burke's style is noble, earnest, deep-flowing, because his

sentiment was lofty and fervid, and went with sincerity
and ardent disciplined travail of judgment. Fox told
Francis Horner that Dryden's prose was Burke's great
favourite, and that Burke imitated him more than any-
one else. We may well believe that he was attracted by
Dryden's ease, his copiousness, his gaiety, his manliness of
style, but there can hardly have been any conscious attempt
at imitation. Their topics were too different. Burke had
the style of his subjects, the amplitude, the weightiness,
the laboriousness, the sense, the high flight, the grandeur,
proper to a man dealing with imperial themes, the freedom
of nations, the justice of rulers, the fortunes of great
societies, the sacredness of law. Burke will always be
read with delight and edification, because in the midst
of discussions on the local and the accidental, he scatters
apophthegms that take us into the regions of lasting wisdom. In the midst of the torrent of his most strenuous
and passionate deliverances, he suddenly rises aloof from
his immediate subject, and in all tranquillity reminds us
of some permanent relation of things, some enduring truth
of human life or society. We do not hear the organ
tones of Milton, for faith and freedom had other notes in
the seventeenth century. There is none of the complacent
and wise-browed sagacity of Bacon, for Burke's were days
of eager personal strife and party fire and civil division.
We are not exhilarated by the cheerfulness, the polish, the
fine manners of Bolingbroke, for Burke had an anxious conscience, and was earnest and intent that the good should
triumph. And yet Burke is among the greatest of those
who have wrought marvels in the prose of our English
tongue.

The influence of Burke on the publicists of the generation after the Revolution was much less considerable than

might have been expected. In Germany, where there has
been so much excellent writing about *Staatswissenschaft,*
with such poverty and darkness in the wisdom of practical
politics, there is a long list of writers who have drawn
their inspiration from Burke. In France, publicists of the
sentimental school, like Chateaubriand, and the politico-
ecclesiastical school, like De Maistre, fashioned a track of
their own. In England Burke made a deep mark on contemporary opinion during the last years of his life, and
then his influence underwent a certain eclipse. The official Whigs considered him a renegade and a heresiarch,
who had committed the deadly sin of breaking up the
party, and they never mentioned his name without bitterness. To men like Godwin, the author of *Political Justice,*
Burke was as antichrist. Bentham and James Mill
thought of him as a declaimer who lived upon applause,
and who, as one of them says, was for protecting everything old, not because it was good but because it existed.
In one quarter only did he exert a profound influence.
His maxim that men might employ their sagacity in dis-
covering the latent wisdom which underlies general prejudices and old institutions, instead of exploding them,
inspired Coleridge, as I have already said ; and the Cole-
ridgian school are Burke's direct descendants, whenever
they deal with the significance and the relations of Church
and State. But they connected these views so closely
with their views in metaphysics and theology, that the
association with Burke was effectually disguised.

The only English writer of that age whom we can name
along with Burke in the literature of enduring power,
is Wordsworth, that great representative in another
and a higher field, and with many rare elements added
that were all his own, of those harmonizing and concilia-

tory forces and ideas that make man's destiny easier to
him, through piety in its oldest and best sense ; through
reverence for the past, for duty, for institutions. He was
born in the year of the *Present Discontents* (1770), and
when Burke wrote the *Reflections*, Wordsworth was standing, with France " on the top of golden hours," listening
with delight among the ruins of the Bastille, or on the
banks of the Loire, to " the homeless sound of joy that
was in the sky." When France lost faith and freedom,
and Napoleon had built his throne on their grave, he
began to see those strong elements which for Burke had
all his life been the true and fast foundation of the social
world. Wide as is the difference between an oratorical
and a declamatory mind like Burke's, and the least orato-
tical of all poets, yet, under this difference of form and
temper, there is a striking likeness in spirit. There was the
same energetic feeling about moral ideas, the same frame
of counsel and prudence, the same love for the slowness of
time, the same slight account held of mere intellectual
knowledge, and even the same ruling sympathy with that
side of the character of Englishmen which Burke exulted
in, as '*their awe of kings and reverence for priests,*'
'*their sullen resistance of innovation,*' '*their unalterable
perseverance in the wisdom of prejudice.*'

The conservative movement in England ran on for many
years in the ecclesiastical channel, rather than among
questions where Burke's writings might have been brought
to bear. On the political side the most active minds,
both in practice and theory, worked out the principles of
liberalism, and they did so on a plan and by methods
from which Burke's utilitarian liberalism and his historic
conservatism were equally remote. There are many signs
around us that this epoch is for the moment at an end.

The historic method, fitting in with certain dominant con-
ceptions in the region of natural science, is bringing men
round to a way of looking at society for which Burke's
maxims are exactly suited; and it seems probable that he
will be more frequently and more seriously referred to
within the next twenty years than he has been within the
whole of the last eighty.

GILBERT AND RIVINGTON, PRINTERS, ST. JOHN'S SQUARE, LONDON.